Our

International

Monetary

System

YESTERDAY, TODAY,

and TOMORROW

STUDIES IN ECONOMICS

CONSULTING EDITOR, DONALD DEWEY

Columbia University

Our International Monetary System

ROBERT TRIFFIN
YALE UNIVERSITY

YESTERDAY, TODAY, and TOMORROW

RANDOM HOUSE / NEW YORK

SECOND PRINTING

© Copyright, 1968, by Random House, Inc.

All rights reserved under International and Pan-American Copyright Conventions.
Published in New York by Random House, Inc. and simultaneously in
Toronto, Canada, by Random House of Canada Limited.

Library of Congress Catalog Card Number: 68-10846

Manufactured in the United States of America
by The Colonial Press Inc., Clinton, Mass.

Design by Diana Hrisinko

TO
*Pierre Teilhard de Chardin
and Jean Charon, and their inspiring vision
of the evolutionary process*

Preface

Let me begin with a bold prediction that should be particularly pleasing to my publishers. The marathon debate on international monetary reform, opened by a few academic writers more than seven years ago and by the officials more than three years ago, will still be raging when this book comes off the printing press. It is even unlikely to be stilled for long by the grand international monetary agreement now anticipated to emerge sometime in 1968. The best that can be hoped from this—as yet hypothetical—agreement is that it will pave the way for an orderly and gradual adaptation of our international monetary institutions to ever-changing needs and conditions. In this field as in others, change is the law of life, and our all too frequent failure to recognize it in time is the main seed of economic disasters as well as of internal revolutions and international wars.

Money, like all other human institutions, is the prey of an evolutionary process that has always eluded the attempt of "conservatives" to stop it, and of "radicals" to deflect it too widely from the trajectory imparted to it by the momentum of past decisions and accidents.[1]

Man's command over his own fate depends both on a broad vision of his goals for the future and on a realistic awareness of the shackles imposed upon his rational planning by past history. These two conditions are only rarely and partly met in fact, and historical developments tend therefore to be molded by unforeseen and haphazard accidents far more than by conscious decisions.

The very birth of money was not only unplanned, but even unnoticed. Early "commodity moneys" gradually evolved out of mere barter transactions, in which some specific commodities emerged as *the* most convenient and generally acceptable counterpart for all other goods and services. The dominance of gold and silver in this role, over many centuries, was not itself, at least initially, the product of any rational decision of any institutional authority, but an evolutionary by-product of individual choices based on the appropriateness of these metals to perform this monetary role, by reason of their intrinsic value, durability, divisibility, and so on.

Legislative interventions by the state authorities certainly assumed an increasing role in later developments of the monetary systems, but were by no means as determining as is often imagined. The most momentous of these developments were indeed totally unforeseen, or even directly contrary to the intentions of the official authorities theoretically in charge.

The displacement of silver by gold, and of both by paper money, in the domestic monetary circulation of all countries was

[1] This "iron law" of evolution, linking the future to the past, extends, of course, beyond man himself to all the other components of the world of which he is only a part. For daring, but illuminating and inspiring, explorations of this time-dimension of our world, see the writings of the two men to whom this book is dedicated, and particularly Pierre Teilhard de Chardin, *The Future of Man* (New York: Harper & Row, 1964), and Jean E. Charon, *L'Etre et le Verbe* (Paris: Planète, 1966) and *Man in Search of Himself* (London: Allyn & Unwin, 1967).

the combined result of legislative or regulatory errors and ignorance, and of spontaneous market developments over which any conscious control or direction by the national authorities developed only very slowly and imperfectly.[2] The same is true of the haphazard and checkered growth of the gold-exchange standard. Its basic instability was dramatically demonstrated by its collapse in 1931 and is still today a matter for great concern and anxiety. Yet, the international agreements necessary for the smooth functioning of an international monetary system still elude us today.

One of the reasons, at least, for such continued frustrations lies in the lack of understanding of the evolutionary requirements of any international monetary institutions adjusted to changing needs and circumstances, outside as well as inside the narrow field of money itself. The simplified and abstract models in which economists attempt to describe, or mold, the complex realities of the living world generally lack the *time dimension,* which is so crucial in this respect. The "gold-standard" model of our textbooks, for instance, is a highly abstract construct, which gives little or no hint of the fundamental changes briefly summarized above, and particularly of the gradual euthanasia of gold money itself and its replacement by paper money as the main circulating medium. Contrary to a widespread mythology, this process had already been largely completed before the eruption of World War I. Similarly, current plans for international monetary reform—including my own—inevitably lay their main stress on immediate policy objectives, but do not always make fully explicit the basic requirement of adaptability to future changes in the economic and political environment to which monetary institutions must continually adjust in order to serve efficiently man's changing goals in an evolutionary world.

[2] This point is brilliantly developed and documented in Jacques E. Martens, *La naissance et le développement de l'étalon-or, 1696–1922* (Louvain and Paris: 1944).

Plan of the Book

It is these evolutionary features that Part I of the present volume tries to emphasize, not for the sake of past history itself, but as a reminder of the lessons that it holds for the present-day reformers of the international monetary system. Its major theme is that the gradual assertion of man's control over his physical environment is marked, in the monetary field, by the gradual displacement of "commodity money" by man-made "fiduciary money." This process has long been completed for money and payments within each country's borders. Its extension across national borders is already far more advanced than most people realize, but continued and orderly progress along this path will require considerable ingenuity and courage on the part of experts and governments for many years to come.

Up to World War I the existence of national borders did not affect significantly the adjustment process to which every issuer of fiduciary money was subjected. The impact of market pressures upon individual banking firms—including central banks—tended to harmonize *ex ante*—and not merely to correct *ex post* —the pace of monetary expansion among them, irrespective of national borders. These pressures were indeed very similar to those that continue today to limit divergent rates of expansion among private banks within each monetary area.

The significance of national borders in the adjustment process derives from governmental interventions, promoting and underwriting such divergent rates of expansion, even at the risk of exchange restrictions or changes in the country's exchange rates. The disturbances introduced thereby in the international trade and payments system have promoted, since World War II, increasing efforts to avoid the worst consequences of economic nationalism. Concerted coordination of national monetary policies should be viewed, in that light, as the only acceptable alternative to an impossible restoration of the nineteenth-century laissez-faire mechanism of international adjustment.

Part I of the book, entirely devoted to the past, should probably be of interest only to students who need to wash from their
brains the half-truths or "mis-truths" of their textbooks. Most
other readers may wish to skip it and turn directly to Chapter 3,
which summarizes the first part of the book and points out its
significance for current reform plans. Conversely, the readers of
Chapters 1 and 2 should skip Chapter 3.

Part II looks at the future, but in the light of the past reviewed in Part I.

Chapter 4 peers into the *long-run* evolution of our international monétary system suggested by past trends as well as by a
purely rational analysis of the needs that such a system should
serve. It abstracts, however, from the limitations imposed upon
such rational planning, at least in the short run, by old entrenched habits of mind and bureaucratic resistance to institutional changes.

Chapter 5 summarizes the three major issues around which
the present debate has organized itself, that is, (1) the proper *use*
of international monetary reserves—as an alternative to "unnecessary" and a complement to "necessary" policy adjustments, (2)
the *amounts and growth rates* of monetary reserves required for
this purpose, and (3) the *composition* of the world reserve pool
—including particularly the agreements that may be needed in
this respect to avoid frustration of the first objective above and
the destabilization impact of sudden shifts from one reserve medium to another.

Chapter 6 reviews the course of the current negotiations
initiated by the formation of the Group of Ten in October, 1963,
but involving also the IMF and the UNCTAD.

Chapter 7 tries to appraise the strength and weaknesses of
the proposals developed so far and to highlight the *convergent*
interests of all concerned as guidelines for a reconciliation of the
conflicting national "negotiating positions" that have barred so
far any agreement on concrete remedies to the agreed defects of
the present system.

Chapter 8 summarizes, for the hurried reader, the main arguments and conclusions of this book.

Confession and Acknowledgments

The publication of this book would have had to wait for many more months of tedious rewriting if I had not been able to draw extensively on three previous publications of mine, which required only minor changes to find their place in an integrated presentation of the problem under discussion:

1. *The Evolution of the International Monetary System: Historical Reappraisal and Future Perspectives* (Princeton, N.J.: Princeton Studies in International Finance No. 12, 1964)

2. "From Waterloo to Tokyo," *The Economist* (London: August 15, 1964)

3. "International Monetary Reform," a study prepared at the request of the United Nations Economic Commission for Latin America and published in the *Economic Bulletin for Latin America* (April, 1966)

I wish to thank the publishers for their kind permission to use this material in this volume, and apologize to my readers for occasional repetitions or overlapping, which I have tried to keep to an unobtrusive minimum.

Robert Triffin

Contents

Preface   *vii*

PART I: THE EVOLUTION OF THE INTERNATIONAL
  MONETARY SYSTEM: 1815–1965

  1. The Gold Standard: Myths and Realities:
    1815–1913   *3*

  THE MECHANISM OF ADJUSTMENT AMONG COUNTRIES   4
  Textbook Abstract   4
  Historical Abstract   5
  Reinterpretation and Conclusions   13
  THE INTERNATIONAL PACE OF ADJUSTMENT   16
  A Gentle Reminder to the Apostles of Gold Money   16
  Monetary Expansion and International Reserves Be-
    fore World War I   21

2. *A Half Century of International Monetary Anarchy: 1914–1965*   29

THE AFTERMATH OF WORLD WAR I   29
THE AFTERMATH OF WORLD WAR II   32
THE MECHANISM OF INTERNATIONAL RESERVE CREATION
   IN THE LAST HALF CENTURY   38
The Mechanism of Adjustment Among *Countries*   39
The International Pace of Adjustment   40

PART II: REFORM PLANS AND NEGOTIATIONS

3. *The Evolutionary Path from Past Monetary Institutions to Future Reforms*   53

THE EUTHANASIA OF GOLD UNDER THE SO-CALLED GOLD
   STANDARD   54
THE AFTERMATH OF WORLD WAR I   55
THE AFTERMATH OF WORLD WAR II   57
EVOLUTION, REVOLUTION, OR REGRESSION?   58

4. *The Long-Run Evolution of Our International Monetary System*   61

BASIC FEATURES   61
A Single Reserve Center   62
Cash Settlements   62
Credit Operations   64
Consolidation of Outstanding Currency-Reserve
   Balances   69
International Guarantees   69
OTHER ISSUES, OBJECTIONS, AND ALTERNATIVES   70
Surrenders of National Sovereignty?   70
Stable versus Fluctuating Rates   72
Whether and When?   75

5. *Three Major Issues: Proper Use, Amount, and Composition of Reserves*   78

THE MUTUAL ADJUSTMENT OF NATIONAL POLICIES   79
Internal Impact   79
External Impact   82
THE CREATION OF WORLD RESERVES   88
Reserve Requirements in an Expanding World Economy   88
The Factors Determining Reserve Creation   95
The Adjustment of Supplies to Needs   98
THE FOREIGN-EXCHANGE COMPONENT OF WORLD
RESERVES   99

6. *The Course of Negotiations on International Monetary Reform*   103

AN EMERGING CONSENSUS   104
NEGOTIATING DIVERGENCES AMONG THE TEN   107
Basic Differences   107
Compromises and Dissents   110
THE IMF PROPOSALS   119
THE REPORT OF THE UNCTAD'S EXPERTS   124

7. *Convergent Interests and Operational Solutions* 130

LONG-RUN OBJECTIVES AND SOLUTIONS   131
The Aggregate Volume of Reserve Creation   131
Participation and Voting Rights   134
Reserve Deposits with the Fund as Source of Fund Financing   136
Pressures for Balance-of-Payments Adjustment, and Their Distribution between Surplus Countries and Deficit Countries   139
Regional Monetary Integration   143
AN URGENT FIRST STEP   146
Arguments for Negotiating Priority   146
Broad Features of Proposed Initial Agreement   148

Negotiability of Such an Agreement   152
Extension to Other Countries   156
Link to Long-Term Objectives   158
On the Relation of the Above Proposals to Other
    Current Proposals for International Monetary
    Reform   161
**Appendix to Chapter 7: Proposed Initial Agreement
    for the Establishment of a Gold Conversion
    Account among Major Gold Reserve Holders**   162

8. Summary and Conclusions   165

The Evolution of National Monetary Systems from
    Commodity Moneys to Fiduciary Money   165
The Evolution of International Monetary Reserves
    from Commodity Reserves to Fiduciary Reserves   168
The International Adjustment Mechanism   170
Negotiating Tactics and Convergent Interests   172
Short-Run Forecasts and Long-Run Perspectives   177

Appendix   181

AN APPEAL TO THE GROUP OF TEN   181
GOING IT ALONE IN MONETARY REFORM   186

POSTSCRIPT   190

The International Monetary Problem after Rio   190

**Selected Bibliography on the Current Debate on
    International Monetary Reform**   197

Index   203

Tables

CHAPTER 1

Table 1.1   *Wholesale Price Indexes, 1814–1913*   **18**

Table 1.2   *The Structure of Money, 1815–1913*   **26**

Table 1.3   *Origin of Money and Reserve Increases, 1816–1913*   **27**

Table 1.4   *Average Yearly Growth Rates of Monetary Gold Stock, Total Money Supply, and "Uncovered" Credit Money, 1816–1913*   **28**

CHAPTER 2

Table 2.1   *Annual Growth Rates and Sources of World Monetary Reserves, 1914–1966*   **42**

Table 2.2   *Structure and Distribution of Monetary Reserves, 1913–1966*   **46**

Table 2.3   *Sources of Reserve Creation, 1914–1966*   **48**

CHAPTER 5

Table 5.1   *Gross Monetary Reserves, Imports, and Money Supply, 1949–1964*   **90**

Table 5.2   *Sources of Gross Reserve Increases, 1960–1966*   **97**

Table 5.3   *Reserve Switches from Foreign Exchange in the First Half of 1965*   **101**

CHAPTER 6

Table 6.1   *Net Fund Positions and Voting Power*   **109**

Table 6.2   *Alternative Criteria for Distribution of Fund Units*   **128**

CHAPTER 7

Table 7.1   *Reserve Composition, 1937–June, 1967*   **149**

Table 7.2   *Maximum Impact of Proposed Gold Conversion Account Agreement upon Direct Gold Holdings of Members*   **153**

PART I

The Evolution of the International Monetary System: 1815-1965

1

The Gold Standard:
Myths and Realities—
1815-1913

The monetary traditions and institutions of the nineteenth century provided a remarkably efficient mechanism of mutual adjustment of national monetary and credit policies to one another, essential to the long-term maintenance of exchange-rate stability between national currencies.

The reasons for this success, and for the breakdown of the system after World War I, are very imperfectly reflected in most of our textbooks. Most of all, however, overconcentration on the mechanism of *intercountry* adjustments fails to bring out the broader forces influencing the *overall pace* of monetary expansion on which individual countries were forced to align themselves.

SOURCE: Reprinted with changes from Robert Triffin, *The Evolution of the International Monetary System: Historical Reappraisal and Future Perspectives* (Princeton, N.J.: Princeton Studies in International Finance No. 12, 1964). Reprinted with permission.

The Mechanism of Adjustment Among Countries

TEXTBOOK ABSTRACT

Starting from an initial position of balance-of-payments equilibrium, the emergence of a fundamental deficit is generally described in terms of divergent movements of exports—downward —and imports—upward—in the deficit countries, with opposite, and equally divergent, movements in the surplus countries.

The money flows associated with the international settlement of such imbalances, if not offset by domestic "neutralization" policies, should then tend to prompt downward price readjustments in the deficit countries, and upward readjustments in the surplus countries. This would restore a competitive price and cost pattern among them, and bring their balances of payments back into equilibrium.

These "automatic" adjustment forces were strengthened and speeded up by central banks through the so-called rules of the game. Discount-rate policy and open-market interventions would raise interest rates and tighten credit in the deficit countries, while lowering interest rates and expanding credit in the surplus countries. This would both (1) cushion balance-of-payments and monetary transfers in the short term by stimulating compensatory capital movements from the surplus to the deficit countries, and (2) accelerate the desirable downward readjustment of prices and costs in the latter countries and their upward readjustment in the first.

The "rules of the game" were widely violated after World War I. The surplus countries adopted "neutralization" policies, which increasingly concentrated upon the deficit countries the burdens of adjustment previously distributed between surplus and deficit countries alike. At the same time, the development of stronger resistance to downward price and wage adaptations— particularly as a result of the growing strength of the trade unions—blocked the price-adjustment mechanism in the deficit countries, transferring its impact to fluctuations in economic activity and employment. The resulting social and political strains gradually became unbearable, particularly during the world depression of the 1930's, and induced governments to abandon the harsh gold-standard disciplines in favor of fluctuating exchange rates and/or trade and exchange restrictions.

HISTORICAL ABSTRACT

This highly simplified digest of the theory of international adjustment under the actual gold standard certainly meets the first test of an economic theory, that is, the test of logical consistency. Does it meet equally well the second test by which a theory should be judged, that is, its conformity to the major facts calling for explanation?

It undoubtedly fits *some* of the facts. Comparative price—or exchange-rate—movements obviously play a role in the fluctuations of balances of payments on current account, and are themselves influenced by the tightening or expansion of money flows arising both from international settlements and from domestic policies or lack of policies.

Other facts, however, must also be taken into account if we are to develop a general and politically meaningful theory of balance-of-payments adjustments.

1. First of all, the most cursory look at international trade statistics reveals an enormous degree of parallelism—rather than divergent movements—between export and import fluctuations *for any one country,* and in the general trend of foreign-trade movements *for the various trading countries.* Over the eighty years from 1880 to 1960, all significant increases or decreases in the exports of Western Europe were marked by *parallel* increases, or decreases, *for the eleven major trading countries of the world* in 91 percent of the cases, and by *simultaneous* increases, or decreases, of *exports and imports for each country,* taken separately, in 88 percent of the cases. These proportions fall to 77 and 73 percent, respectively, for fluctuations of one year only, but rise to 95 and 92 percent for fluctuations of more than a year's dura-

tion, and to 98 and 100 percent for movements extending over more than four years.[1]

2. Equally impressive is the overall parallelism—rather than divergence—of price movements, expressed in the same unit of measurement, between the various trading countries maintaining a minimum degree of freedom of trade and exchange in their international transactions. In spite of wide differences and fluctuations in the composition of each country's exports, the indexes of export unit values—measured in current dollars—for the same eleven countries over the period 1870–1960 moved in the same direction in 89 percent of the observed fluctuations, and in opposite direction in only 11 percent of the cases.[2]

This solidarity of national price movements—when measured in a common unit of account—is not incompatible, of course, with sharp divergences in national price levels, offset by opposite divergences in exchange-rate fluctuations. One does find indeed that any large variations in the evolution of national prices are invariably offset, more or less rapidly, by exchange-rate fluctuations, and vice versa. Such variations were, however, eschewed—except in wartime—by most industrial countries in the nineteenth century, but were relatively frequent in the countries of the so-called periphery, and particularly in Latin America.

3. Third, downward wage adjustments rarely reached any sizable amplitude, even in the nineteenth century, among the countries that maintained exchange-rate stability, and it may be doubted whether they would have proved much more acceptable at that time, economically, politically, and socially, than they are today. Wherever substantial inflation had been allowed to develop, international cost competitiveness was nearly invariably

---

[1] The above percentages are derived from 287 observations of national increases or decreases for eleven countries (the United States, the United Kingdom, France, Germany, Italy, Belgium, the Netherlands, Switzerland, Sweden, Austria, and Canada), in the course of seventeen upward or downward movements of more than one percent in Western European exports, in the period 1880–1960. The estimates used in these calculations are those of Angus Maddison, "Growth and Fluctuations in the World Economy," *Banca Nazionale del Lavoro Quarterly Review* (June, 1962), pp. 179–181.

[2] Based on estimates from the same source, pp. 189–190.

restored through devaluation rather than through downward price and wage adjustments.

Standard statistical series for the United States, the United Kingdom, France, and Germany show only four or five instances of actual declines in any broad-based indexes of money wages during the fifty years preceding World War I. Such declines were, moreover, usually confined to one or a few percentage points only. They were far exceeded, in post-gold-standard days, by the much sharper wage drops of the 1920–1922 recession—37 percent in the United Kingdom—and of the first years of the great depression—22 percent in the United States and Germany.[3]

4. The "neutralization" policies stigmatized by Ragnar Nurkse as another major cause—alongside of increasing price and wage rigidity—of the downfall of the gold standard[4] were by no means a postwar innovation. Using exactly the same techniques of measurement as Nurkse, Arthur I. Bloomfield found that "central banks in general played the rules of the game just as badly before 1914 as they did thereafter!"[5] It might be noted in passing, however, that Nurkse's method defines as neutralization the cases where fluctuations in a central bank's domestic portfolio offset only a fraction—no matter how small—of the changes in its international assets. In many cases, however, there remained a *positive* correlation between the latter and changes in the central bank's sight liabilities. The impact of the latter changes upon the country's money supply would most often be magnified, in turn, several times by the operation of the private banking system under customary cash and liquidity requirements. Nurkse's "neutralization" policies, therefore, could still

[3] See, for instance, *Historical Statistics of the United States* (Washington, D.C.: Bureau of the Census, 1960), pp. 90–92; B. R. Mitchell, *Abstract of the British Historical Statistics* (Cambridge: Cambridge University Press, 1962), pp. 343–345; and France's *Annuaire Statistique—1938* (Paris: 1939), pp. 443–444.

[4] See Ragnar Nurkse, *International Currency Experience* (League of Nations, 1944), pp. 66–88.

[5] Arthur I. Bloomfield, *Monetary Policy under the International Gold Standard: 1880–1914* (New York: Federal Reserve Bank of New York, 1959), p. 50. The evidence of neutralization, measured by Nurkse's formula, was present in 60 percent of total observations, in the period 1880–1913, coinciding exactly with Nurkse's results for the 1922–1938 period.

permit a *multiple* impact of international gold—or foreign-ex-change—movements upon money supply, as contrasted with the mere one-to-one impact that would have resulted under the pure gold-coin system of monetary circulation assumed in the most ab-stract formulations of gold-standard theory.[6]

5. The impact of discount rates on *cushioning* capital move-ments and on *corrective* changes in cost competitiveness was also far less general and uniform than is usually assumed.

The first seems indeed to have been particularly effective for the well-developed money and capital markets of the major creditor countries and financial centers, and most of all in the case of the United Kingdom. Discount and interest-rate changes could accelerate, or slow down, the normal, or average, pace of capital exports, and had to be resorted to frequently by the Bank of England to defend its very slender gold reserves. The much higher reserve levels of the Bank of France enabled it, on the other hand, to cushion temporary deficits out of its own reserves, with much rarer recourses to discount-rate changes. Most of all, however, capital-importing countries were far less able to influ-ence in the same way the pace of their capital imports, these being primarily determined by the ease or stringency prevailing in the major financial centers.

The impact of Britain's international surpluses and deficits on British bank reserves was cushioned, moreover, by the ample use of sterling balances as cash reserves by overseas banks, par-ticularly throughout the British Empire. Surpluses and deficits between Britain and its Empire—and even, to some extent, with other countries—merely led to a reshuffling of British bank de-posits, rather than to an overall expansion or contraction in their amount and to correlative gold inflows or outflows.

Finally, the enormous role played by the London discount market in the financing of the food and raw-materials exports of the less-developed countries probably imparted to the Bank of England's discount-rate policy an influence on British terms of

---

[6] See Robert Triffin, "National Central Banking and the International Economy," *International Monetary Policies,* Postwar Economic Studies, No. 7 (Washington, D.C.: Board of Governors of the Federal Reserve System, 1947), pp. 52–53.

trade—and balance of payments—which has escaped the attention of economic theorists. Increases in discount rates did, indeed—as is usually pointed out—tend to reduce British prices and costs, improving the competitiveness of British exports in world markets and of homemade import-substitute goods on the domestic market. What is forgotten, however, is that the tightening of the London discount market also affected, most directly and overwhelmingly, the ease with which inventories of staple foods and raw materials could be financed, thus forcing also a quicker liquidation and attendant price declines in Britain's chief import goods. Such declines could be expected to be far larger than those in the less sensitive and volatile prices of British industrial exports. Thus, the favorable impact of discount-rate increases on British competitiveness (lowering British prices in relation to foreign prices in competing industrial nations) would be reinforced in its balance-of-payments effects by a simultaneous improvement of Britain's terms of trade (that is, by decreases in the prices of foreign suppliers of complementary goods to Britain, larger than the decreases in British export prices to them).[7]

6. The importance of international capital movements, and of their fluctuations, is often obscured by the disproportionate emphasis often placed on comparative price and cost fluctuations as the major factor in balance-of-payments disequilibria and their correction. Attention is thereby centered on the current-account items of the balance of payments, and tends to suggest that most disturbances arose in this area and had to be corrected promptly by the restoration of equilibrium between receipts and expenditures on current—or even merely merchandise—account.

In fact, however, international capital movements often did cushion—and even stimulate—vast and enduring deficits, or surpluses, on current account without calling for any correction whatsoever, except in an extremely long run indeed. Developing

[7] See Robert Triffin, "National Central Banking and the International Economy," pp. 60–63; and Peter B. Kenen, *British Monetary Policy and the Balance of Payments* (Cambridge, Mass.: Harvard University Press, 1960), pp. 59–62, and especially the chart on p. 60.

countries, such as the United States, Canada, Argentina, Australia, and so on, could maintain, over an average of years, large and persistent deficits on current account, financed by correspondingly large, persistent, and growing capital imports from the more advanced countries of Western Europe. Rough estimates, compiled by the United Nations,[8] place at about $40.5 billion, on the eve of World War I, the gross long-term foreign investments of the principal creditor countries of Western Europe, and at $3.5 billion those of the United States. Of this $44 billion total, $12 billion had been invested in Europe itself, $6.8 billion in the United States—which was still a net debtor country at the time—$8.5 billion in Latin America, $6.0 billion in Asia, $4.7 billion in Africa, $3.7 billion in Canada, and $2.3 billion in Australia and New Zealand.

The lion's share of these investments was that of the United Kingdom ($18 billion), followed by France ($9 billion), and Germany ($5.8 billion). The United Kingdom had indeed been running persistent and growing surpluses on current account for more than a century, without any tendency whatsoever toward equilibrium. On the contrary, these surpluses rose continually from about $35 million a year, on the average, over the years 1816–1855, to more than $870 million a year in the last years before World War I (1906–1913). Nobody could ever dream of explaining this favorable balance—and its fluctuations—in terms of the cost-competitiveness adjustment mechanism depicted in the textbooks, since it arose primarily from Britain's earnings on its swelling foreign-investment portfolio, and coincided with large and increasing *deficits* on merchandise account—close to $670 million a year over the period 1906–1913—offset themselves, for the most part, by net receipts on services and remittances account.

These current-account surpluses were nearly fully absorbed by Britain's investments abroad, which rose over the same period from an average of less than $30 million a year in 1816–1855 to more than $850 million a year in 1906–1913, and indeed more

[8] *International Capital Movements during the Inter-War Period* (New York: United Nations, 1949), p. 2.

than a billion dollars a year in the last three prewar years, that is, about a third of the British export level at the time, and 10 percent of net national income.[9]

Foreign investments on such a scale undoubtedly accelerated economic development and helped at times relieve balance-of-payments pressures in the recipient countries. In the case of the United States, for instance, net capital inflows from Europe—primarily Britain—financed large and growing deficits on current account throughout most of the nineteenth century. They reached a peak of close to $300 million in 1888, tapering off afterward, and shifting to net capital exports around the turn of the century, as the United States finally turned from chronic deficits to equally chronic surpluses on current account.[10]

7. The cyclical pattern of international capital movements, however, had a very different impact upon the capital-exporting and the capital-importing countries.

A mere slowdown of capital exports could help relieve, in the first countries, any pressures on central-bank—and private-bank—reserves arising from unfavorable developments in other balance-of-payments transactions. In the British case, for instance, capital exports dropped year after year, from their 1872 peak of roughly $480 million to $60 million in 1877, recovered again to $480 million in 1890, and declined once more in the following years to $110 million in 1898, rising nearly uninterruptedly afterward to $250 million in 1904, and booming to $400 million in 1905, $570 million in 1906, to reach finally close to $1100 million in 1913.[11]

The borrowing countries, on the other hand, were far less able to control the rate of their capital imports, which tended, on the whole, to swell in boom times and dry up in hard times, contributing further to the economic instability associated with their frequent dependence on one or a few items of raw material

[9] The above estimates are derived from Albert H. Imlah, *Economic Elements in the Pax Britannica* (Cambridge, Mass.: Harvard University Press, 1958), Table 4, pp. 70–75.

[10] See *Historical Statistics of the United States*, pp. 562–566.

[11] See Albert H. Imlah, *Economic Elements in the Pax Britannica*, pp. 73–75.

or foodstuff exports, themselves subject to wide quantity and/or price fluctuations. All in all, therefore, the balance of payments of the countries of the so-called periphery would be assisted over the long run by the large capital imports available to them from the financial markets of industrial Europe, but these countries would pay for this dependence through perverse fluctuations in the availability of such capital and in their terms of trade over the cycle. The exchange-rate instability of most underdeveloped countries—other than those of colonial or semicolonial areas tightly linked to their metropolitan country's currency and banking system—finds here one of its many explanations.[12]

8. Another important qualification of the traditional theory of balance-of-payments adjustments relates to the international timing of reserve movements and discount-rate changes. The textbook explanation suggests that rate increases were undertaken by the deficit countries in order to relieve a drain of their reserves to the surplus countries. As noted by Bloomfield, however,

> the annual averages of the discount rates of twelve central banks [England, Germany, France, Sweden, Finland, Norway, Denmark, Belgium, Switzerland, the Netherlands, Russia, and Austria-Hungary] reveal the . . . interesting fact that, in their larger movements at least, the discount rates of virtually all the banks tended to rise and fall together. . . . To some degree, and certainly for many of the banks, this broad similarity reflected competitive or "defensive" discount rate changes. . . . But a more important explanation lies in the fact that discount rates in most . . . of the individual countries tended . . . to show a positive correlation, though generally not a very marked one, with domestic business cycle fluctuations. Since, as is well known, major cyclical fluctuations tended to be broadly synchronous in all countries, discount rate movements thus generally tended to exhibit a broad parallelism over the course of the world cycle—although there were, of course,

[12] Another, closely connected with the main topic of this study, lies in the retention of a silver standard long after the effective abandonment of silver or bimetallic standards in Europe and the United States.

many dissimilarities with respect to short-term movements in the various countries.[13]

This importance of parallel movements, associated with the international business cycle—as against divergent movements between surplus and deficit countries—brings us back to the first two points made above (pp. 5–6) and to the comparative neglect of this parallelism in textbook discussions centered nearly exclusively on intercountry balance-of-payments adjustments.

REINTERPRETATION AND CONCLUSIONS

1. The nineteenth-century monetary mechanism succeeded, to a unique degree, in preserving exchange-rate stability—and freedom from quantitative trade and exchange restrictions—over a large part of the world.

2. This success, however, was limited to the more advanced countries, which formed the core of the system, and to those closely linked to them by political, as well as economic and financial ties. The exchange rates of other currencies—particularly in Latin America—fluctuated widely, and depreciated enormously, over the period. This contrast between the "core" countries and those of the "periphery" can be largely explained by the cyclical pattern of capital movements and terms of trade, which contributed to stability in the first group, and to instability in the second.

3. The adjustment process did not depend on any tendency toward equilibrium of the national balances of payments on current account. Vast and growing capital movements cushioned over many years, up to a century or more, correspondingly large and increasing surpluses—and deficits—on current account.

4. The preservation of exchange-rate stability depended, however, on the impact of international monetary settlements—of the combined current and capital accounts—upon domestic monetary and credit developments. Large or protracted deficits

[13] *Monetary Policy under the International Gold Standard: 1880–1914*, pp. 35–37.

or surpluses had to be corrected, residually, by a slowdown or acceleration of bank-credit expansion sufficient to bring about—through income and/or price and cost adaptations, and their impact on exports and imports—a tenable equilibrium in overall transactions, and a cessation of persistent drains in the deficit countries' stock of international money (that is, gold and silver initially, and increasingly gold alone as all major countries shifted from the silver or bimetallic standard to the gold standard).

5. This residual harmonization of national monetary and credit policies depended far less on *ex post* corrective action, requiring an extreme flexibility, downward as well as upward, of national price and wage levels, than on the *ex ante* avoidance of substantial disparities in cost competitiveness and in the monetary policies that would allow them to develop.

As long as stable exchange rates were maintained, national *export* prices remained strongly bound together among all competing countries, by the mere existence of an international market not broken down by any large or frequent changes in trade or exchange restrictions. Under these conditions, national price and wage levels also remained closely linked together internationally, even in the face of divergent rates of monetary and credit expansion, as import and export competition constituted a powerful brake on the emergence of any large disparity between internal and external price and cost levels.

Inflationary pressures could not be contained within the domestic market, but spilled out *directly,* to a considerable extent, into balance-of-payments deficits rather than into uncontrolled rises of internal prices, costs, and wage levels.[14] These deficits led, in turn, to corresponding monetary transfers from the domestic banking system to foreign banks, weakening the

---

[14] This is still true today, in the absence of major changes in exchange rates and/or trade and exchange restrictions. See Robert Triffin and Herbert G. Grubel, "The Adjustment Mechanism to Differential Rates of Monetary Expansion Among the Countries of the European Economic Community," *Review of Economics and Statistics* (November, 1962), pp. 486–491, reproduced in my book on *The World Money Maze: National Currencies in International Payments* (New Haven: Yale University Press, 1966), pp. 29–38.

cash position of domestic banks and their ability to pursue expansionary credit policies leading to persistent deficits for the economy and persistent cash drains for the banks. (Banks in the surplus countries would be simultaneously subject to opposite pressures, which would also contribute to the harmonization of credit policies around levels conducive to the reequilibration of the overall balance of payments.)

Central banks could, of course, slow down this adjustment process by replenishing through their discount or open-market operations the cash reserves of the commercial banks. As long as exchange controls or devaluation were effectively ruled out from their horizon, however, they would themselves be responsive to similar pressures, arising from the decline in the ratio of their own reserves to liabilities. While their liabilities were internal, and thus easy to expand, their reserves were—and still are today—limited to international assets over which they had no direct control.

6. These pressures for international harmonization of the pace of monetary and credit expansion were indeed very similar in character to those which continue today to limit divergent rates of expansion among private banks within each national monetary area.

They were further reinforced, as far as central banks were concerned, by the fact that a substantial portion of the domestic monetary circulation itself was in the form of commodity money —gold and silver—wholly or partly international in character, rather than in credit money. Expansionary credit policies were thus accompanied by an outflow of gold and silver assets from the coffers of central banks into internal circulation and commercial banks' reserves, as well as to foreign countries. This movement of specie into internal circulation was all the more pronounced, as the lowest denomination of paper currency was usually much too high—often equivalent to several times the level of monthly wages—to be usable in household and wage payments. Central-bank credit expansion was therefore limited not only by *foreign* deficits and gold losses, but also by *internal* gold and silver losses, very much as commercial banks' credit and deposit expansion

may be limited today by the drain on their paper-currency reserves. While the latter can be replenished by central-bank credit,
central banks themselves did not have access to any gold or silver
"lender of last resort."

The overall pace of advance of commercial banks' credit
and deposit-money creation in a national economy was and remains subject today to the policies of the central bank. Similarly, the *overall* pace of credit creation by the central banks *as
a group* was limited, in the nineteenth century's international
economy, by their ability to increase *simultaneously* their international reserves.

7. This latter observation brings once more into the lime-
light a most important question left unanswered by the theory
of balance-of-payments adjustment among countries: granted the
need for mutual harmonization of national monetary policies
among the gold-standard countries, what were the factors determining the *international pace* on which such alignments did
take place? The question is all the more significant in view of
the size and parallelism of major fluctuations in national price,
export, and import levels over the period 1815–1914 as a whole.

The International Pace of Adjustment

A GENTLE REMINDER TO THE APOSTLES OF GOLD MONEY

1. The gold standard is often credited with having reconciled, to an unprecedented degree, price stability with a high rate
of economic growth over the nineteenth century. Contemporary
advocates of a return to gold rarely miss the opportunity of quot-
ing, in this respect, Gustav Cassel's observation that "the general
level of prices in 1910 was practically the same as in 1850." [15]
This stability is then attributed to the safeguards erected against
inflation by the small size of new gold production and monetary

[15] Gustav Cassel, "The Supply of Gold," in *Interim Report of the Gold Delegation of the Financial Committee* (Geneva: 1930), p. 72. The calculation is based
on the Sauerbeck-Statist index of wholesale prices, and carried back to 1800 on
the basis of Jevons' index. See also, in the same report, Joseph Kitchin, "The
Supply of Gold Compared with the Prices of Commodities," pp. 79–85.

gold increases in relation to existing stocks, and, more generally and optimistically, to the response elasticity of new gold production to any substantial decreases or increases in the price level: price declines or increases would be kept in check by their impact on gold-mining costs and profitability, and the resulting stimulation or slowdown of new gold production and monetary expansion.

2. As pointed out by Cassel himself, however, price fluctuations were by no means inconsiderable in the nineteenth century. Increases and decreases of 30 to 50 percent, or more, accompanied the famous Kondratieff cycles,[16] and have been attributed by many writers—including Cassel—to fluctuations in gold production, following new mining or refining discoveries.

The evidence of long-term stability—or rather reversibility —of prices seen in the return of the 1910 index to its 1850 level is, to say the least, extremely misleading. Such an arbitrary choice of dates would allow us, for instance, to demonstrate equally well the "stability" of the price level over the period from 1913 to the early 1930's, since the precipitous fall of prices during the Great Depression brought back both the United States and the United Kingdom price indexes down to approximately their 1913 level in 1931–1932!

The starting point of Cassel's comparison—1850—is taken close to the very bottom of a long depression during which prices had fallen by 50 percent or more, while the end year—1910— comes at the end of a fifteen-year upward trend during which the index used by Cassel had risen by more than 30 percent.

Making the same comparison from peak to peak, or from trough to trough, we would find a rather pronounced downward long-run trend of wholesale prices in all major countries (see Table 1.1). Prices declined, for instance, by 25 percent in the United States from 1814 to 1872, and by 25 percent again from 1872 to 1913, adding up to a cumulative 44 percent decline over the century, from 1814 to 1913. In the United Kingdom, price de-

[16] See N. D. Kondratieff, "Die langen Wellen der Konjunktur," *Archiv für Sozialwissenschaft* (December, 1926), abridged in English by W. Stolper, "The Long Waves of Economic Life," *Review of Economics and Statistics* (November, 1935).

clines of 30 percent from 1814 to 1872, and 20 percent from 1872 to 1913, also add up cumulatively to a similar 44 percent decline for the century as a whole.

Table 1.1   Wholesale Price Indexes, 1814–1913

	United States	United Kingdom	Germany	France	Italy
Indexes (1913 = 100)					
1814	178	178	129	132[1]	
1849	80	90	71	96	
1872	133	125	111	124	
1896	67	76	71	71	74
1913	100	100	100	100	100
Changes (in %)					
1814–1849	−55	−49	−45	−27[2]	
1849–1872	+66	+39	+56	+31	
1872–1896	−50	−39	−36	−43	
1896–1913	+49	+32	+41	+41	+35
1814–1913	**−44**	**−44**	**−22**	**−24[2]**	

NOTES:
1. 1820
2. since 1820

SOURCES:
1. *For the United States:*
   a) Warren and Pearson index until 1890
   b) BLS index since 1890
2. *For the United Kingdom:*
   a) Gayer, Rostow, and Schwartz index until 1849
   b) Rousseaux index from 1844 to 1871
   c) Board of Trade index since 1871
3. *For Germany, France, and Italy: Annuaire Statistique de la France,* pp. 513–515 of 1951 edition (Paris: Institut National de la statistique générale de la France, 1952)

3. The influence of fluctuations in gold production upon these broad price trends seems far more plausible than the supposed inverse relationship from commodity prices to gold production. The significance of any such relationship as may have existed was certainly dwarfed by the gold avalanche unleashed by the discovery of new gold fields and the improvement of mining and refining techniques, both after 1848 and after 1888. On both occasions, current production just about doubled, over twenty-

four or twenty-five years, the gold stock accumulated over the previous three and a half or four centuries. The yearly rate of growth in the estimated *monetary* gold stocks—after deduction for hoarding, industrial, and artistic uses—rose abruptly from 0.7 percent in the first half of the nineteenth century to 4.3 percent over the years 1849–1872, declined precipitously to only 1.3 percent in 1873–1888, and rose again to 3.2 percent in 1889–1913.

4. The neat mechanistic explanation derived by some authors from this broad parallelism between gold production and long-run trends in commodity prices fails, however, to give a full account of the complex factors involved in the process of nineteenth-century economic growth. The Kondratieff long waves were certainly influenced also to a major degree by the clustering and spread of technological discoveries and innovations in production, transportation, and so on, by the vast migrations from old to new settlement areas, and—last but not least—by the preparation, waging, and aftermath of wars. These powerful influences, brilliantly analyzed by Schumpeter[17] among others, obviously cannot be reduced to any mechanistic monetary explanation. It would be equally absurd, on the other hand, to deny that monetary and banking developments also had a role—even if primarily permissive, rather than initiating—on the acceleration or retardation of price trends and production growth. Schumpeter himself insisted abundantly on the role of bank credit in the process of capitalistic development.

One might well wonder, indeed, whether the unprecedented stability of the major currencies in terms of gold—and exchange rates—in the nineteenth century was not due to the spectacular growth of bank money or "credit money"—in the form of paper currency and bank deposits—rather than to the residual, and fast declining, role of gold and silver "commodity money." Certainly, full dependence of the monetary system on gold and silver, in pre–nineteenth-century days, to the exclusion or near-ex-

[17] Joseph A. Schumpeter, *The Theory of Economic Development* (Cambridge, Mass.: Harvard University Press, 1934), and *Business Cycles* (New York: McGraw-Hill, 1939).

clusion of credit or paper money, did not prevent wide inflation-ary excesses—through debasement of the coinage—and wide fluc-tuations in exchange rates. The pound sterling lost three fourths of its gold value and the French franc more than nine tenths, from the middle of the thirteenth century to the end of the eighteenth century.

5. It is rather ludicrous to reflect that the vast literature de-voted to the so-called nineteenth-century gold standard is prac-tically devoid of any quantitative estimates of the enormous changes that modified, out of all recognition, the actual structure of the volume of money, or means of payments, as between gold, silver, currency notes, and bank deposits, between the end of the Napoleonic wars and the outbreak of World War I.

According to the League of Nations estimates, paper cur-rency and bank deposits already accounted in 1913 for more than 85 percent of overall monetary circulation in the world, and gold for only 10 percent. Comprehensive estimates for earlier periods are practically nonexistent and can only be pieced together from disparate sources, the reliability of which is most difficult to as-sess. Yet, some broad facts and orders of magnitude can hardly be in doubt. Bank currency and demand deposits probably consti-tuted less than a third of total money supply at the beginning of the nineteenth century, but eight to nine tenths of it by 1913. Silver exceeded gold in actual circulation by about two or three to one until well into the second half of the century, but dropped considerably behind in the latter part of the period, the previous proportion being just about reversed by 1913. Increases in credit money—paper currency and demand deposits—accounted, in the major and more developed countries, for two thirds or more of total monetary expansion after the middle of the century, and about 95 percent from 1873 to 1913 (see Tables 1.2 and 1.3 at the end of this chapter).

These facts can hardly be reconciled with the supposed *automaticity* still ascribed by many writers—particularly in Eu-rope—to the so-called nineteenth-century gold standard. The reconciliation of high rates of economic growth with exchange-rate and gold-price stability was made possible indeed by the rapid growth and proper management of bank money, and could hardly have been achieved under the purely, or predominantly, metallic systems of money creation characteristic of the *previous* centuries. Finally, the term "gold standard" could hardly be applied to the period as a whole, in view of the overwhelming dominance of silver during its first decades, and of bank money during the latter ones. All in all, the nineteenth century could be far more accurately described as the century of an emerging and growing credit-money standard, and of the euthanasia of gold and silver moneys, rather than as the century of the gold standard.

MONETARY EXPANSION AND INTERNATIONAL RESERVES
  BEFORE WORLD WAR I

A more precise assessment of the nature of the nineteenth-century international monetary mechanism and of its relation to production and price fluctuations must await the development of better monetary and reserve statistics than are now available, not only for the world as a whole, but even for the major countries which formed the basic core of the so-called gold standard. The task should not prove impossible, if two limitations are accepted from the start. The first relates to the dearth of meaningful and reasonably reliable statistics for many countries. This should not prove too damaging for an appraisal of the international monetary mechanism in the few major countries which formed in the nineteenth century—and still form today—the core of the system. I have assembled some rough estimates of this sort, running back to 1885, for eleven such countries (the present so-called Group of Ten, or Paris Club, including Switzerland). They accounted in 1885 and 1913 for 60 to 80 percent of the world money supply and monetary reserves. Earlier estimates—back to 1815—are for three countries only—the United States, the United Kingdom, and France—but accounted for about half the world money and reserves in 1885 and 1913, and for about two thirds to three fourths of the eleven core countries.

The second limitation lies in the incompleteness and lack of full comparability of available data even for the major countries. Yet, this could hardly be more damaging than similar—and often far worse—limitations on the validity of other nineteenth-century estimates, in the field of national accounting for instance. They certainly remain, moreover, very minor in relation to the broad orders of magnitude involved in the enormous shifts in the monetary structure revealed by the tables presented at the end of this chapter.[18] In any case, imperfect as they are bound to be, such estimates are essential to an understanding of the nineteenth-century international monetary mechanism and far better than the implicit and totally unwarranted assumptions that underlie most of past and current theorizing about the so-called gold standard.

With these qualifications in mind, the following observations can be derived from these estimates:

1. Although the 1816–1848 estimates are particularly venturesome, there can be no doubt about the very slow growth of monetary gold stocks—just about nil, if we can trust the estimates—and of total money supply—about 1.4 percent a year—over this period. Monetary expansion was sustained, not by gold accretions, but by an approximate doubling of silver stocks, accounting for about two thirds of the total increase in the money supply, and for the remaining third by the incipient increase in internal credit monetization.[19]

2. The gold avalanche of the next twenty-four years produced an average increase of 6.2 percent yearly in the total stock of monetary gold. This rate of growth declined sharply, to about 1.4 percent a year, from 1873 to 1892, but recovered to about 3.6 percent in the last twenty years preceding the outbreak of World War I. (See Table 1.4.)

These enormous fluctuations in gold-stock increases were sig-

[18] For further details and comments, see Appendix I (pp. 51–63) of my Princeton study in *The Evolution of the International Monetary System: Historical Reappraisal and Future Perspectives* (Princeton, N.J.: Princeton University Press, 1964).

[19] The latter being measured, indifferently, by the excess of money supply increases over the increase of monetary gold and silver stocks, or by the excess of credit money increases over the increase of monetary reserves.

nificantly smoothed down by concurrent adaptations in the functioning of the monetary and banking system. The yearly rate of growth of money supply declined only from 4.2 percent in 1849–1872 to 3.3 percent in 1873–1892, and recovered to 4.3 percent, on the average, in the period 1893–1913. (See Table 1.4.)

This smoothing down was due, to a minor extent, to the partial offsetting of gold fluctuations by opposite fluctuations in the monetary silver stocks. These contracted substantially in the two periods of fastest gold expansion, but more than doubled during the leaner gold years from 1873 through 1892. Far more significant is the dwarfing of gold and silver stock changes by the spectacular growth of credit money, which fed more than 70 percent of total money increases over the years 1849–1872, and about 95 percent throughout the rest of the period. (See line IA3 of Table 1.3.)

3. Credit money—that is, paper currency and bank deposits —did not, however, normally circulate beyond the national borders of the issuing country and banking institutions. Exchange-rate stability thus depended on their ready convertibility—directly by the issuing banks, or ultimately through a national central bank—into the foreign currencies required, or into metallic currencies or bullion of international acceptability. Silver bullion lost its previous role in this respect around 1872, and silver-coin settlements remained acceptable only among the countries of the Latin Monetary Union. Silver, however, was no longer "full-bodied" money, as the commercial value of silver coins fell well below their nominal value.[20] Gold thus emerged increasingly as the primary guarantor of international exchange stability even for the countries which remained on a so-called limping bimetallic standard.

Three factors explain the maintenance of stable exchange

---

[20] The valuation of silver at nominal par in the tables thus *understates* the importance of credit money, since silver coinage included in effect a substantial credit money component. Its acceptance at par among the countries of the Latin Union demonstrates the feasibility of international credit money settlements, even under the very imperfect arrangements negotiated to this effect among the countries of the Latin Union.

rates in the face of growing issues of *national* credit moneys, side by side with fast declining proportions of *international* gold and silver moneys.

The first is the *de facto* harmonization of the national rates of monetary and credit expansion among the gold-standard countries. This harmonization itself, however, depended, as pointed out above (pp. 14–15), on the reaction of the issuing banks to the fluctuations in their reserve ratio arising from cyclical movements in internal circulation, as well as from external settlements of balance-of-payments disequilibria.

The *overall pace* of expansion, in turn, could not but be strongly influenced by the ability of the national banking systems to accumulate sufficient gold reserves to guarantee the convertibility of their national credit money issues into the gold through which foreign currencies could be acquired at stable exchange rates. The maintenance of relatively fast rates of monetary expansion after 1848 was thus conditioned by two further factors which the tables at the end of this chapter bring clearly into light.

The first was the spectacular spurt in gold production that followed the discovery of new gold fields and improved mining and refining techniques, and was of course predominantly accidental in character.

The second lay in the resiliency and adaptability of monetary and banking institutions, and the enormous economy of the precious metals that resulted from their increasing transfers from actual circulation in the public to the reserve coffers of commercial banks and of national central banks—or Treasury in the case of the United States.[21] The proportion of monetary gold and silver stocks absorbed in centralized monetary reserves rose from about 10 percent in 1848 to 16 percent in 1872, 41 percent

[21] The reserve estimates of the tables refer to the centralized holdings of central banks and treasuries only. The gold and silver components of money supply estimates include, therefore, gold and silver held by other issuing banks and commercial banks, thus overstating once more the metallic component of money supply in the modern sense of the word—coin, currency, and demand deposits in the hands of the public—and understating the proportion of credit money in circulation outside banks.

in 1892, and 51 percent in 1913.[22] Even more significant is the relative proportion of new gold accretions absorbed by central reserves, on the one hand, and by the public and banks on the other. During the first gold avalanche of 1849–1872, 81 percent of the new gold was dispersed among the public and banks, only 19 percent being accumulated in reserves. These proportions were nearly exactly reversed in the leaner gold years from 1873 through 1892, 82 percent of the new gold feeding the increase of central reserves, with a multiple impact on overall money creation. When gold production rose again at a faster pace in the period 1893–1913, the proportion absorbed by central reserves declined to 66 percent, while that of private holdings rose from 18 to 34 percent. (See Table 1.3.)

These spectacular changes in the structure of money and reserves thus contributed powerfully both to the maintenance of relatively fast rates of monetary expansion, and to a considerable smoothing out of money supply fluctuations in relation to fluctuations in the available gold stocks.

4. There was nothing inherently stable, however, in a process of monetary creation so heavily dependent on the accidents:

a. of gold and silver discoveries and production rates;

b. of uncoordinated—and largely irrational—national decisions regarding the adoption, retention, or abandonment of silver, gold, or bimetallism as the basic monetary standard;

c. of compensatory adaptations in banking structure, the scope of which would inevitably taper off over time, especially when central banks could no longer replenish their own reserves from the dwindling—relatively, if not yet absolutely—amounts of gold still in circulation.

In any case, the slow evolution, which had gradually adjusted the international monetary system of the nineteenth

---

[22] The proportion of gold alone temporarily dropped from 31 percent in 1848 to 20 percent in 1872, rising later to 35 percent in 1892 and 51 percent in 1913. The 1848–1872 decline, however, was more than compensated by the increased absorption into centralized reserves of silver, which could still be regarded at that time as a valid reserve component. After 1872 the movements of gold alone are more significant than those of gold and silver combined.

century to the economic requirements of peacetime economic growth, but had also changed it out of all recognition between 1815 and 1913, was brutally disrupted by the outbreak of World War I. The ensuing collapse of the system ushered in half a century of international monetary chaos, characterized by widespread exchange-rate instability and/or trade and exchange controls, with only brief interludes of nostalgic and vain attempts to fit upon the twentieth-century economy the monetary wardrobe of the nineteenth-century world.

Table 1.2   The Structure of Money, 1815–1913
(in percentage of total money supply)

End of Year	1815	1848	1872	1892	1913	1913 II	1913 III
I. Commodity money	67	63	41	24	13	15	17
A. Gold	33	17	28	16	10	10	10
B. Silver	34	46	13	9	3	5	7
II. Credit money	33	37	59	76	87	85	83
A. Currency	26	20	32	22	19	22	25
B. Deposits	6	17	27	54	68	63	59
III. Total (I + II) in billions of United States dollars	1.0	1.6	4.3	8.1	19.8	26.3	33.1

NOTES:

1. The first five columns give combined estimates for the United States, the United Kingdom, and France. The sixth column (II) covers, in addition, the other countries of the current so-called Group of Ten (Germany, the Netherlands, Italy, Belgium, Sweden, Switzerland, Canada, and Japan). The last column (III) gives rougher estimates for the whole world.

2. As might be expected, the proportion of deposits in total money supply declines slightly in the last two columns, while that of currency notes and silver coinage increases, as the coverage is enlarged by the inclusion of less advanced countries.

3. For sources and other comments on this and the following tables, see pp. 51–55 of my study on *The Evolution of the International Monetary System: Historical Reappraisal and Future Perspectives* (Princeton N.J.: Princeton University Press, 1964).

Table 1.3 Origin of Money and Reserve Increases, 1816–1913

Period	1816–1913	1816–1848	1849–1872	1873–1892	1893–1913	1886–1913		
						I	II	III
I. In % of money increases								
A. Money increases	100	100	100	100	100	100	100	100
1. Gold	9	−9	34	2	6	4	5	4
2. Silver	2	65	−6	3	—	−1	1	−4
3. Credit money	90	44	72	95	94	97	94	100
a. Currency	19	8	39	12	17	16	20	23
b. Deposits	71	37	33	83	77	80	74	77
B. Reserve increases	14	14	8	27	11	13	16	21
1. Gold	11	11	8	10	12	11	13	16
2. Silver	3	3	—	17	−1	2	1	3
3. Foreign exchange						—	2	3
C. Total gold and silver increases	25	70	36	33	17	17	20	18
1. Gold (A1 and B1)	20	1	42	12	18	16	18	19
2. Silver (A2 + B2)	5	69	−6	21	−1	1	2	−1
D. Internal credit monetization (A3 − B = A − B3 − C)	75	30	64	67	83	83	78	79
II. Percentage of absorption of new gold into:								
A. Reserves	56	886	19	82	66	71	72	78
B. Circulation	44	−786	81	18	34	29	28	22

NOTE:

1. The last three columns give, for comparison's sake, available estimates for the eleven-country group (II) and for the world (III) as well as for the three countries (I) covered in the preceding columns.

Table 1.4   Average Yearly Growth Rates of Monetary Gold Stock, Total
Money Supply and "Uncovered" Credit Money, 1816–1913
(in percentages)

Period	1816–1848	1849–1872	1873–1892	1893–1913	1886–1913		
					I	II	III
I. Monetary gold stock	0.1	6.2	1.4	3.6	2.6	2.8	2.5
II. Total money supply	1.4	4.2	3.3	4.3	4.2	4.2	3.1
III. "Uncovered" credit money	1.4	6.5	4.0	5.4	5.5	5.5	4.3

NOTES:

1. See note to Table 1.3 above.

2. "Uncovered" credit money includes only the portion of credit money in excess of total gold and silver reserves. It is also equal, by definition, to the excess of the money supply over the total of monetary gold and silver stocks, whether in reserves or circulation.

3. The increase in the monetary silver stocks over the periods 1816–1848 (2 percent yearly) and 1873–1892 (4 percent), and its decline (by one percent yearly, or less) over the periods 1849–1872 and 1893–1913, also contributed to smoothing down the impact of changes in the monetary gold stock upon the total money supply.

2

A Half Century of

International Monetary

Anarchy: 1914-1965

The Aftermath of World War I

The financing of World War I and of postwar reconstruction forced, as has always been the case in previous and later wars, sharp and inflationary increases in the monetary liabilities of national banking systems, while gold production expanded at a much slower rate than previously. The ratio of gold reserves to money supply—and foreign trade—thus fell drastically, well below the levels compatible with the maintenance of convertibility in most of the belligerent countries. Convertibility was suspended over a large part of the world.

Freely fluctuating exchange rates failed signally, in the following years, to restore a competitive price and cost pattern among the major trading nations, to induce the adoption of monetary policies compatible with even a moderate degree of stability in prices and exchange rates, and to bring about any sort of tenable equilibrium in the world's balance-of-payments pattern. They stimulated instead speculative movements of hot money which contributed to a considerable overvaluation of the pound sterling—at its old prewar parity—to a parallel under-valuation of the French and Belgian francs, to an utter collapse of the German mark, and to various degrees of overvaluation and undervaluation in the bilateral relationships among these and other currencies.

Currency convertibility was finally restored, in one country after another, in the second half of the 1920's, but under condi-tions that could not fail to usher in its early collapse, after a brief period of euphoria in some countries and of unendurable hardships in others.

First of all, the outflow of hot money from the European continent to Britain led to the adoption of fundamentally under-valued exchange rates in the first countries and of an overvalued rate in the latter, thus unleashing strong expansionary forces on the continent, but a deep slump in exports, economic activity, and employment in Britain.

Secondly, the return to convertibility had to be sustained by the reconstruction of adequate reserve levels by the central banks. This was achieved in the undervalued countries with the help of foreign loans, of the revaluation of the outstanding gold and for-eign-exchange assets of central banks at the new gold and foreign-exchange parities,[1] and of the large balance-of-payments sur-pluses stimulated by the undervaluation itself.

A substantial component of these surpluses, however, was constituted by the return of refugee capital from London, under the triple impact of currency stabilization and booming eco-nomic activity on the continent, and of the deep economic slump in Britain. The reconstruction of adequate reserve levels in Brit-ain, on the other hand, had been achieved very largely on the basis of these previous inflows of continental hot money, and was now severely threatened both by its repatriation to the home countries and the attraction of Wall Street.

[1] French gold and foreign-exchange reserves, for instance, rose from 5.5 billion old francs in 1927 to 64.7 billion new francs in 1928, 87 percent of the total increase arising from the nominal revaluation profits resulting from the redefi-nition of the franc parity.

The British authorities were by no means unaware of the vulnerability of this position, and had long prepared two lines of defense to protect it. One was the agreement between Benjamin Strong, president of the Federal Reserve Bank of New York, and Montagu Norman, governor of the Bank of England, to try and preserve higher interest rates in Britain than in the United States. The agreement became harder and harder to implement, however, in the face of the British slump and of the boom on Wall Street. The other line of defense was the attempt of Britain to propagandize the adoption—by other countries—of a so-called gold-exchange standard under which their central banks would hold a substantial portion of their international monetary reserves in the *national* currency of major trading and financial centers, that is, very largely in sterling. This succeeded, for a while, in shoring up Britain's slender gold reserves against the impact of speculative capital withdrawals, following the stabilization of European currencies. Central-bank reserves of foreign exchange rose from about $700 million in 1913 to more than $3 billion in 1928, of which some $2½ billion—that is, three to four times the total gold reserves of England—may be estimated to have been held in sterling, legally convertible into gold on demand or on very short notice.

The Bank of France, however, showed itself increasingly reluctant to continue to retain as a permanent component of its reserves the whole amount of the sterling balances that it had to buy from the market in order to prevent a further appreciation of the French franc, after its sharp rise from 260 francs to 125 francs per pound in the latter part of 1926. Conversions of official French holdings of sterling into gold or dollars became a growing source of worry for the Bank of England, which had to plead also with other countries to refrain *voluntarily* from converting their gold-convertible sterling into gold.

The financial sequels—particularly in Germany and Central Europe—of the 1929 world crisis finally swept away the fragile convertibility façade, so painfully restored in the late 1920's. Convertibility was once more suspended in Britain, on September 21, 1931, ushering in long years of international monetary chaos, compounded by the great depression of the 1930's, World War II and its aftermath, and the worldwide spread of exchange-rate instability, exchange control, and bilateralism.

The Aftermath of World War II

The monetary aftermath of World War II presents a number of contrasts to, but also a striking similarity with, that of World War I.

Once again, wartime and postwar reconstruction financing brought about vast increases in money supply and a considerable decline in the ratio of international reserves to national monetary liabilities. Generalized recourse to exchange controls slowed down, or postponed, the exchange-rate readjustments that had characterized the 1920's, and bunched up many of them in September, 1949. In spite of the 1949 devaluations, however, the ratio of gold reserves to money supply for the eleven major countries of the Paris Club, taken as a group, fell from about 39 percent in 1937 to 19 percent in 1949.

The pound sterling was, this time, engulfed also in the devaluations that swept the other European currencies. Its international status as a reserve currency had never fully recovered from the 1931 collapse, and had been weakened further by the forced or semiforced accumulation of inconvertible pounds by many countries, during and after the war. Refugee capital had flown, not to London, but to New York, contributing in the end to a long-term undervaluation of the European currencies in general in terms of the mighty postwar United States dollar.

Central banks once more accumulated a growing portion of their international reserves in the form of foreign exchange, alongside of gold metal, but this accumulation centered now on the dollar rather than the pound. The reserve liabilities of the United States to foreign monetary authorities rose from about $0.8 billion in 1939 to $8.7 billion in 1957 and $16.1 billion in 1966.

The gradual undermining of the United States net reserve position from nearly $23 billion in 1949 to about $16 billion in

1957 took a more precipitous turn with the huge United States balance-of-payments deficits of the later years, when the effects of the relative undervaluation of the European currencies were compounded by the reflux of European refugee capital, following the restoration of currency confidence and convertibility in Europe. Net United States reserves declined by more than a half, from $16 billion to $7 billion, between the end of 1957 and the end of 1960.

The latent dollar crisis burst into the open in October, 1960, with the sudden flare-up of gold prices on the London market.[2] The reversal of short-term private-capital movements has continued, ever since, to exercise a heavy drag on our overall balance of payments. Normal inflows averaging $500 million a year in the early 1950's and about $1 billion a year in the late 1950's were replaced by persistent outflows of more than $2 billion in 1960, and about $1.6 billion in each of the following two years.[3]

The gold drain from the United States was kept at tolerable levels by the accumulation of dollar balances by foreign central banks, but as these continued to pile up the United States authorities had, like Britain some thirty years earlier, to try and elicit, through bilateral and multilateral discussions and negotiations, voluntary restraints on the conversion into gold of the gold-convertible dollar balances accumulated by foreign central banks under the ill-fated gold-exchange standard. Continuous efforts had to be devoted also to eliciting international cooperation in discount and interest-rate policies—as had also been hammered out in a reverse direction between Benjamin Strong and Montagu Norman in the late 1920's—so as to moderate short-term capital

[2] The influence of the cessation of U.S.S.R. sales, and of other accidental factors, was sharply aggravated by the sudden withdrawal of the Bank of England from the market, following dark hints by our own Treasury officials that the support operations of the Bank might not fall within the scope of "legitimate monetary purposes" conditioning central banks' access to the United States Treasury gold.

[3] See also Robert Triffin, "The Latent Crisis of the Reserve Currencies," *The Banker* (London: August, 1963), reproduced in *The World Money Maze*, pp. 102–118.

outflows from New York to the European markets. Once more, such policies proved harder and harder to impose, or preserve, in the face of national economic conditions calling for an exactly opposite pattern of interest rates, in Europe as well as in the United States.

In brief, the contrast between financial and economic developments in the United States and in Europe after World War II closely resembles the previous contrast between developments in the United Kingdom and in continental Europe after World War I:

1. In the early postwar years, large movements of private capital and central-bank funds from Europe to the United States;

2. The consequent undervaluation of European currencies in relation to the dollar, when a new and durable pattern of exchange rates emerged, in September, 1949, under the influence of such capital movements;

3. The resulting stimulation of exports and economic activity in Europe, and downward pressures on growth rates and employment in the United States;

4. The repatriation of European refugee capital, under the double impact of (2) and (3), after the restoration of confidence in European currencies;

5. The acceleration of United States capital outflows and reserve losses, prompted by speculative expectations of possible changes in gold prices and exchange rates, as well as by the differential evolution of earning prospects and interest rates in Europe and in the United States under the impact of (2) above;

6. The growing conflict between domestic and external criteria governing the choice of credit and interest-rate policies, on both sides of the Atlantic; and the predictable frustration of European attempts to persuade the United States authorities to raise interest rates in the face of heavy unemployment, as well as of American attempts to persuade Eu-

ropean authorities to lower interest rates in the face of heavy inflationary pressures at home;

7. The United States efforts to elicit further purchases and retention of dollar balances by foreign central banks, and to discourage conversions of such balances into gold or foreign currencies;

8. Protracted discussions and negotiations on the need to remedy the gold—or liquidity—shortage and the instability inherent in the haphazard accumulation and liquidation of foreign-exchange reserves under the gold-exchange standard.

There remain, fortunately, major differences between the British monetary problem in the aftermath of World War I and the United States problem today.

First of all, the world economy is in far better shape today than it was in 1931, and the overall economic and financial position of the United States is far stronger than that of 1931 Britain.

Second, the world's financial and political leaders are now keenly aware of the disastrous consequences which any repetition of the 1931 policies, or lack of policies, could entail for the international monetary and economic order of the West. They have also developed since World War II deeply ingrained habits of cooperation in vital matters and laid the foundations, at least, of the worldwide and regional monetary institutions necessary to organize, on a durable basis, the functioning of an international monetary system adapted to the realities of the financial, economic, and political interdependence of their theoretically sovereign countries.

These two basic differences have so far allowed us to ward off a tragic repetition of the international monetary crisis unleashed in September, 1931 by the collapse of sterling, which soon engulfed a gold-exchange standard in which sterling then played a major role. A similar crisis of a gold-exchange standard in which the United States dollar now plays the dominant role might have been triggered as early as 1960 by the sudden flare-up of gold prices in London in October of that year. It elicited, instead, unprecedented efforts at international monetary cooperation in two different, but complementary, directions, which will be discussed in greater detail in Part II of this volume.

The first consisted essentially in shoring up the existing system through a variety of short-term arrangements, involving a wide array of mutual credit lines between central banks, both on a bilateral basis and within the existing framework of the International Monetary Fund. The major steps in this direction were as follows:

1. The *ad hoc* reserve operations repeatedly undertaken by central banks in favor of sterling in March, 1961; March, 1962; November, 1964; September, 1965; and June, 1966;

2. The formation of the so-called gold pool in the winter of 1961 to coordinate the transactions of major central banks on the London gold market;

3. The sale of so-called Roosa bonds—nonmarketable Treasury bonds and notes, most of which denominated in the currency of the creditor country—to foreign central banks, which reached a peak in mid-1965, declining substantially in later months;

4. Federal Reserve reciprocal currency arrangements and commitments, now totaling more than $5 billion;[4]

5. Sharp increases in IMF quotas from a total of $9.2 billion at the end of 1958 to $21.0 billion as last reported (September, 1967);

6. The "General Arrangements to Borrow" negotiated in 1961–1962 among the so-called Group of Ten (United States, United Kingdom, Canada, Japan, Germany, France, Italy, the Netherlands, Belgium, and Sweden) to make available to the IMF additional resources, up to a theoretical ceiling of $6 billion,[5] in the scarce currencies of major surplus

---

[4] Operations under these agreements are summarized twice a year in reports prepared by Charles A. Coombs and published in the March and September issues of the *Federal Reserve Bulletin*, beginning in September, 1962.

[5] Since the agreement is primarily designed to cushion dangerous capital movements *between* the signatories themselves, the *maximum* resources callable could not, however, exceed half of the total, and are most unlikely to reach even that figure. For further analysis and criticism of this agreement, see my "Lendemains

countries "when supplementary resources are needed to fore-stall or cope with an impairment of the international monetary system . . . in the new conditions of widespread convertibility, including greater freedom for short-term capital movements;"

7 . Last, but not least, the periodical review, in the Monetary Committee of the European Economic Community and in Working Party No. 3 of the OECD [Organization for Economic Cooperation and Development], of developments and policies bearing on the balance-of-payments and monetary stability of the member countries, individually and as a group.

Considerable success was achieved thereby in offsetting and discouraging the speculative capital movements that have threatened, ever since October, 1960, the two key currencies—sterling and particularly the dollar—on which the international gold-exchange standard is anchored. On the other hand, most of the commitments described above remain of a short-term character, subject to frequent renegotiation, and aim only at warding off future crises in the international monetary system, rather than at eliminating the basic vulnerability of the system which is at the root of such crises.[6]

The need to eradicate such vulnerability through more basic reforms of the international monetary system was hotly denied by the official authorities at first, but implicitly acknowledged at the October, 1963, Annual Meeting of the IMF. Pierre-Paul Schweitzer, managing director of the fund, announced in his opening statement that: "In the coming year the Fund will develop and intensify its studies regarding international liquidity, the functioning of the international monetary system, and the

de Vienne: Mesures conservatoires et germes d'avenir," *Trois Etudes sur le problème des liquidités internationales* (Brussels: Banque Nationale de Belgique, April, 1962), pp. 15 and 16.

[6] For a more detailed review of the measures briefly summarized in the above text, see the excellent study of Robert Z. Aliber, *The Management of the Dollar in International Finance* (Princeton Studies in International Finance, No. 13, Princeton: International Finance Section, Princeton University Press, June, 1964).

effective role of the Fund in this field." A few days later, Douglas Dillon, Secretary of the Treasury of the United States, issued a "Statement on Behalf of the 'Group of Ten' Members of the Fund," in which the ministers and Central Bank governors of the ten countries announced the launching of a high-level and "thorough examination of the outlook for the functioning of the international monetary system and of its probable future needs for liquidity." [7] The progress to date of this second, and more momentous, venture in international monetary cooperation will be reviewed in Part II of this volume.

The Mechanism of International Reserve Creation in the Last Half Century

The century that closed with World War I had witnessed the gradual displacement of *international* commodity money (gold and silver) by *national* fiduciary moneys (bank currency and deposits) circulating only within each country's borders. This process was brought to its final completion in the 1920's and early 1930's with the universal disappearance of gold (and full-bodied silver coinage) from active monetary circulation and even from the cash reserves of commercial or deposit banks.

International money—in the form of gold, silver having long lost its previous status in this respect—survived only in the reserves of national central banks, ultimately charged with the task of assuring the free convertibility, at stable exchange rates, of the national currency into the foreign currencies needed for settlements across the country's borders, and vice versa. An adequate stock of international monetary reserves thus became a crucial link for the preservation of a smoothly functioning international payments system among several scores of national fiduciary currencies.

The fundamental revolution in the world monetary structure entailed by this nationalization of money brought in its wake

---

[7] See *Summary Proceedings,* Annual Meeting, 1963, International Monetary Fund, pp. 30 and 285–286.

equally radical transformations in the double mechanism of adjustment reviewed in Chapter I above, that is, (1) the mechanism of adjustment among countries, and (2) the international pace of adjustment.

THE MECHANISM OF ADJUSTMENT AMONG COUNTRIES

The mechanism of adjustment *among* countries, previously distributed among the many banking firms engaged in the issuance of currency and deposits, now centered upon the national monetary authorities themselves. These national monetary authorities, moreover, were able to escape the market pressures which the threat of bankruptcy formally imposed upon each issuer of fiduciary money, legally convertible at par into gold or silver moneys. Previous laissez-faire policies gave way, everywhere, under the pressures of the world war, of postwar reconstruction needs, and of the great depression, and were replaced by interventionist policies involving widely divergent paces of monetary and credit expansion in different countries. Consequent balance-of-payments deficits and reserve losses by the more expansionist —or less contractionist—countries were no longer constrained by an ironclad determination to preserve exchange freedom and stability. These would be sacrificed at times, and resort taken to exchange restrictions or devaluation, when other policy objectives, or mismanagement, led to an excessive depletion of the country's stock of international reserves (see pp. 14–15 above).

The pace of monetary and credit expansion had thus ceased to be harmonized internationally by market pressures acting upon each banking firm, irrespective of national borders. These pressures continued to operate within each national monetary area, but now allowed, or even elicited, widely divergent rates of expansion between one area and another. Such divergencies, when not corrected in time, inevitably led, sooner or later, to the suspension of either exchange freedom or exchange stability or both, with a tendency for currency depreciation and exchange restrictions to spread from one country to another and to aggravate the difficulties of all.

These dire consequences of the monetary nationalism that

characterized the interwar period and the first decade after World War II have, at long last, been taken to heart by national governments and their economic experts. The creation of the International Monetary Fund, the Organization for European Economic Cooperation, the European Payments Union, the GATT [General Agreements on Tariff and Trade], the European Economic Community, and so on, heralded the efforts to reconstruct an international trade and payments system worthy of that name.

The restoration of an international adjustment mechanism can hardly be achieved today, however, through a return to nineteenth-century laissez-faire, that is, through the withering of policy-making and harmonization at the national level. It must perforce entail concerted efforts to enlarge the horizon of policy makers, and to maximize the effectiveness of national policies by making them mutually compatible and supporting, rather than incompatible and mutually defeating. This is the historical significance of the unprecedented development, since the last war, of international monetary and economic consultation, cooperation, and even integration, both at the worldwide and at the regional levels.[8]

THE INTERNATIONAL PACE OF ADJUSTMENT

The international pace of adjustment, for all countries taken together, had increasingly come to depend, even before World War I, on the ability of banking institutions to supplement by fiduciary money the largely haphazard contributions of gold and/ or silver moneys to the expansion of money supply required to sustain the growth of the world economy itself (see pp. 24–25 above). As noted in the concluding paragraphs of Chapter 1, p. 25, "the scope of these compensatory adaptations in banking structure . . . would inevitably taper off over time, especially when

---

[8] One of the latest, but potentially most significant, expressions of this trend is the recent report of Working Party No. 3 of OECD, *The Balance-of-Payments Adjustment Process* (Paris: OECD, August, 1966). See also the academic counterpart of the official report in William Fellner, Fritz Machlup, Robert Triffin, and eleven others, *Maintaining and Restoring Balance in International Payments* (Princeton: Princeton University Press, 1966).

central banks could no longer replenish their own reserves from the dwindling—relatively, if not yet absolutely—amounts of gold still in circulation." Gold coinage had dropped already to about 17 percent of the money supply for the world as a whole by 1885, and to 10 percent by 1913. The withdrawal of remaining gold coin from circulation increased central bank reserves by about $3 billion over the period 1914–1933, contributing about 19 percent of gross reserve increases over the period as a whole, but drying up definitely this traditional source of world reserves growth.

The disappearance of gold coinage from active circulation left the process of money creation—essential to economic growth —entirely dependent upon the expansion of national, fiduciary moneys by the national banking system of each country. Such expansion, however, required in turn a satisfactory rate of expansion of the monetary reserves available to central banks to offset temporary fluctuations in their countries' balances of payments. The amounts of reserves needed to that effect, for the world as a whole, obviously bore only the vaguest of relations, if any, to the supplies of monetary gold determined by the hazards of gold discovery, of gold-mining and gold-refining profitability, and of private gold absorption by industry, the arts, hoarding, and speculation (see pp. 95–96 below). In actual fact, new gold production fed only a rapidly declining fraction of world reserve increases. From about 83 percent of such reserves increases over the years 1886–1913, it fell to 39 percent in 1914–1928 and to 15 percent in 1929–1933 (line II A1, of Table 2.1).

Fiduciary reserves—in the form of gold-convertible so-called key currencies, that is, primarily fiduciary money issues of the United States and the United Kingdom—thus began to supplement gold reserves in the international monetary system of each country. The spread of the gold-exchange standard in the 1920's, however, was as haphazard as the previous spread of the gold standard itself. It was not the product of concerted international decisions, but arose primarily from uncoordinated and highly precarious decisions of scores of central bankers attracted by the earning of interest on dollar and sterling reserves or influenced

Table 2.1   Annual Growth Rates and Sources of World Monetary Reserves, 1914–1966

Period	1914–1928	1929–1933	1934–1937	1938–1949	1950–1959	1960–1964	1965	1966
I. *Annual growth rate*, in percentage of stock at beginning of each period	6.9	9.4	7.9	4.3	2.3	3.7	2.0	1.8
II. *Sources of growth*, in percentage of total for each period	100	100	100	100	100	100	100	100
A. World monetary gold	70	128	83	54	44	26	18	−7
1. Western production minus private absorption	39	15	78	55	33	10	−12	−7
2. Coin withdrawal	31	6	—	—	—	—	—	—
3. Dollar devaluation	—	107	—	—	—	—	—	—
4. Soviet sales	—	—	5	−1	11	16	30	—
B. IMF and BIS transactions	x	x	x	1	7	9	148	4
C. Reserve currencies	30	−28	17	45	49	65	−66	103
1. Dollars	7	−7	5	14	62	50	3	−76
2. Pounds ⎱	23	−20	12	27	−2	7	−24	57
3. Unspecified ⎰				4	−11	7	−46	122

SOURCES AND NOTES:
See Tables 2.2 and 2.3 at the end of this chapter.

by the fact that the reconstitution of satisfactory reserve levels after the war was dependent, for a number of countries, on the negotiation of so-called stabilization loans, or other credits, on the London and New York markets. International palavers, at the Brussels and Geneva conferences, and in the Financial Committee and Gold Delegation of the League of Nations, underwrote the practice—viewed with particular favor by Britain as a way to increase and protect its own slender reserve levels—but failed in their efforts to institutionalize and consolidate it through formal international agreements and commitments. The foreign gold-convertible fiduciary currencies accumulated as reserves by central banks remained subject to sudden and massive cashing into gold, at any time, by their holders at the central bank or Treasury of the debtor countries, that is, primarily the United Kingdom and the United States.

The vulnerability of such a system was dramatically demonstrated by the collapse of sterling, on September 21, 1931, and the consequent near-liquidation of the foreign-exchange component of world monetary reserves. The accumulation of foreign-exchange assets as reserves had contributed about 30 percent of gross reserve increases over the years 1914–1928. Their subsequent liquidation would have brought about a nearly equivalent contraction in overall reserve levels if it had not been made up from other sources, and particularly from the dollar devaluation, which accounted, by itself, for more than the total reserve increases of the years 1929–1933 (lines II C and II A3 of Table 2.1).

The devaluation of the two major reserve currencies discouraged, for a while, the use of foreign currencies as international reserves, while expanding considerably at the same time the gold-metal reserves available to central banks, not only from the spur given to gold production by the increase in gold prices, but also from the disgorging ($2 billion) of previously hoarded gold and from the upward revaluation, in terms of currencies, of existing gold stocks and of physical accretions to them from current production and dishoarding. The share of gold in reserve increases recovered, in the years 1934–1937, to just about the same level (83 percent) as in the heyday of the prewar gold standard (line II A of Table 2.1).

World War II and its aftermath brought, however, a near-repetition, on a vastly expanded scale, of the experience of World War I and its aftermath. The contribution of Western gold production to reserve increases fell again from 78 percent in 1934–1937 to 55 percent in 1938–1949, 33 percent in 1950–1959, 10 percent in 1960–1964, and *minus* 12 and 7 percent respectively in 1965 and 1966 (line II A1 of Table 2.1).

Increasing sales of Soviet gold in Western markets offset only fractionally this declining trend of gold contributions to overall reserve increases, even though such sales accounted in recent years for the bulk of—and in 1965 for more than—the total increase in the noncommunist world's monetary gold stock. They ceased abruptly in 1966 (line II A4 of Table 2.1).

One half to two thirds of postwar reserve growth has been derived from the renewed accumulation by central banks of *national* key currencies as *international* reserves, the primary role in this respect being now assumed, however, by the dollar rather than the pound. The greater financial and economic strength of the United States and the development of international monetary cooperation—spurred in part by the memory of the 1931 collapse—have allowed the system to survive recurrent crises over the years 1960–1964. The year 1965, however, witnessed, for the first time in more than thirty years, a dramatic contraction in the accumulation of reserve currencies. In the first half of the year, the central banks of countries other than the two reserve centers converted into gold ($1.8 billion) and gold-value guaranteed IMF claims ($1 billion) more than $2.7 billion of their past and current accumulation of foreign-exchange holdings. The same movement continued during the following year, with switches from foreign exchange into gold ($2.5 billion) and IMF claims ($2.6 billion) totaling close to $5.1 billion over the two years 1965 and 1966. While the increase in IMF claims in 1966 was largely due to the increase in Fund quotas during that year, that decision itself was, of course, designed to make possible further progress toward internationally concerted reserve creation.

The gold accumulation of countries other than reserve centers in 1965 and 1966 exceeded ten times the world accretions of new monetary gold from current production—minus private absorption—and U.S.S.R. sales. Nearly all of it was derived from the gold losses of the reserve centers, mostly, in fact, the United States.

The preservation of overall reserve expansion in 1965 and 1966, even at sharply reduced rates—2.0 percent or less instead of 3.7 percent, on the average, over the preceding five years—was primarily the result of a spectacular increase in the third—

and newest—component of world reserves, that is, the reserve positions of member countries in the IMF. These increased, for the world as a whole, by $2.2 billion over these two years, as compared with total reserve increases of only $2.9 billion; and for countries other than the two reserve centers, by $2.6 billion, compared with total reserve increases of $3.6 billion.

Taking again a long-term historical view, these developments in the international reserve system closely parallel the previous evolution in national monetary systems, in which fiduciary money gradually displaced gold and silver moneys, but had to be underwritten and consolidated at a later stage through the growth of central banks, acting as lenders of last resort. The IMF is still in its infancy in that respect, but the rapid development of its interventions over recent years may help pave the way for the fundamental reforms that will allow it to provide needed reserve increases in the future and to orient *both* their overall volume and their actual distribution among member countries in such a way as to promote and support national and international policies reconciling monetary stability with feasible rates of expansion in world trade and production.

Table 2.2 Structure and Distribution of Monetary Reserves, 1913–1966 (in billions of United States dollars)

End of	1913	1928	1933	1937	1949	1959	1964	1965	1966
I. World's gross reserves	4.8	13.0	20.4	27.7	45.5	57.3	68.4	69.8	71.1
A. Monetary gold	4.1	9.9	19.3	25.3	35.0	40.2	43.1	43.3	43.2
1. Countries	4.1	9.9	19.3	25.3	33.5	37.9	40.9	41.9	40.9
2. International organizations	x	x	—	—	1.5	2.3	2.2	1.4	2.3
B. Reserves created by IMF and BIS	x	x	—	—	0.2	0.9	2.0	4.0	4.1
1. Reserve positions in IMF	x	x	x	x	1.7	3.3	4.2	5.4	6.3
2. IMF-BIS gold (−)	x	x	—	—	−1.5	−2.3	−2.2	−1.4	−2.3
C. Foreign exchange	0.7	3.2	1.1	2.4	10.4	16.2	23.4	22.5	23.8
II. Net reserves of reserve centers	0.8	1.3	7.3	14.6	17.3	7.6	−5.7	−6.8	−8.7
A. Gold	1.5	4.5	8.4	16.9	25.9	22.0	17.6	16.3	15.2
B. Net claims on IMF	x	x	x	x	1.4	1.6	−0.5	−2.1	−2.6
1. Reserve positions	x	x	x	x	1.5	2.1	0.8	0.6	0.3
2. Liabilities (−)	x	x	x	x	−0.1	−0.5	−1.3	−2.7	−2.9
C. Net foreign exchange	−0.7	−3.2	−1.1	−2.4	−10.0	−16.0	−22.8	−21.0	−21.3
1. Assets	—	—	—	—	0.4	0.2	0.6	1.5	2.5

2. Liabilities (−)	−0.7	−3.2	−1.1	−2.4	−10.4	−16.2	−23.4	−22.5	−23.8
a. Dollars	—	−0.6	−0.1	−0.4	−3.0	−10.4	−16.0	−16.0	−15.1
b. Sterling	−0.7	−2.6	−1.1 }	−1.7	−6.4	−6.2	−7.1	−6.7	−7.5
c. Unspecified	{			−0.2	−0.9	0.4	−0.4	0.3	−1.3
III. Gross reserves of other countries	3.4	8.5	12.0	10.7	17.7	33.0	49.5	51.3	53.1
A. Gold	2.7	5.4	10.9	8.4	7.6	15.9	23.3	25.6	25.8
B. Reserve positions in IMF	x	x	x	x	0.2	1.2	3.4	4.8	6.0
C. Foreign exchange	0.7	3.2	1.1	2.4	10.0	16.0	22.8	21.0	21.3

SOURCES AND NOTES:

1. These estimates have been derived from a variety of official publications, particularly of the League of Nations, the International Monetary Fund, the Board of Governors of the Federal Reserve System, the Bank of England, and the Bank for International Settlements. They involve, especially for the earlier years, rough personal estimates aiming at improving comparability with current, and presumably better, estimates.

2. Note that line I is *not* the sum of lines II and III, but only of lines IIA + IIB1 + IIC1 + III. Lines IA2, IC, and IIC are equal, with reverse sign, to lines IB2, IIC2, and IIIC, respectively.

3. "Unspecified" foreign-exchange reserves (line IIC2c) have been derived residually by deducting from reported foreign-exchange reserve assets (line IC) reported liabilities of the two major reserve centers (the United States and the United Kingdom) to foreign monetary authorities. While part of them are due to various errors and omissions (including some liabilities of other countries), a larger portion probably also represents dollar and sterling claims of central banks held indirectly through the Euro-currency market. They have been grouped, therefore, with other monetary liabilities of the reserve centers on line IIC2.

4. For further comments on pre-1949 estimates, see my study *The Evolution of the International Monetary System: Historical Reappraisal and Future Perspectives* (Princeton, N. J.: Princeton University Press, 1964), p. 67.

Table 2.3　Sources of Reserve Creation, 1914-1966
(Annual rates, in billions of United States dollars)

Periods	1914–1928	1929–1933	1934–1937	1938–1949	1950–1959	1960–1964	1965–1966
I. World's gross reserves	0.5	1.5	1.8	1.5	1.2	2.2	1.3
A. Monetary gold	0.4	1.9	1.5	0.8	0.5	0.6	0.1
1. Western sources	0.2	0.2	1.4	0.8	0.4	0.2	-0.1
a. Production	0.4	0.4	0.9	1.0	0.9	1.3	1.4
b. Absorption (-)	-0.2	-0.2	0.5	-0.1	-0.6	-1.1	-1.6
2. Soviet sales	—	—	0.1	—	0.1	0.3	0.2
3. Coinage withdrawal	0.2	0.1	—	—	—	—	—
4. Dollar devaluation	—	1.6	—	—	—	—	—
B. IMF and BIS transactions	x	—	—	—	0.1	0.2	1.0
1. Gold sales	x	—	—	-0.1	-0.1	—	-0.1
2. IMF reserve liabilities	x	x	x	0.1	0.2	0.2	1.1
C. Foreign exchange	0.2	-0.4	0.3	0.7	0.6	1.4	0.2
1. Dollars	—	-0.1	0.1	0.2	0.7	1.1	-0.5
2. Sterling	0.1	-0.3	0.2	0.4	—	0.2	0.2
3. Unspecified				0.1	-0.1	0.2	0.4
II. Net reserves of reserve centers	—	1.2	1.8	0.2	-1.0	-2.7	-1.5
A. Gold	0.2	0.8	2.1	0.7	-0.4	-0.9	-1.2
B. Net claims on IMF	x	x	x	0.1	—	-0.4	-1.0
C. Net foreign exchange	-0.2	0.4	-0.4	-0.6	-0.6	-1.4	0.7
III. Gross reserves of other countries (= A + B + C = D + E)	0.3	0.7	-0.3	0.6	1.5	3.3	1.8
A. Gold	0.2	1.1	-0.6	-0.1	0.8	1.5	1.2
B. IMF	x	x	x	—	0.1	0.4	1.3
C. Foreign exchange	0.2	-0.4	0.3	0.6	0.6	1.4	-0.7

Table 2.3   (continued)

Periods	1914–1928	1929–1933	1934–1937	1938–1949	1950–1959	1960–1964	1965–1966
D. Net reserve losses of reserve centers ($-$II)	—	-1.2	-1.8	-0.2	1.0	2.7	1.5
1. United States	-0.1	-0.7	-1.4	-0.9	1.2	2.1	0.5
2. United Kingdom	0.1	-0.5	-0.5	0.6	-0.1	0.4	0.5
3. Unspecified	—	—	0.1	0.1	-0.1	0.2	0.4
E. Other sources	0.4	1.9	1.5	0.8	0.6	0.6	0.3
1. World gold (IA)	0.4	1.9	1.5	0.8	0.5	0.6	0.1
2. IMF-BIS transactions *minus* IMF lending to U.S. and U.K.	x	—	—	—	—	—	0.2

SOURCES AND NOTES:
See Table 2.2.

PART II

Reform Plans
and Negotiations

3

The Evolutionary Path

from Past Monetary Institutions

to Future Reforms

Ever since the end of World War I, monetary experts and central bankers have bent their energies on a Proustian "Recherche du Temps Perdu," trying to recapture the lost paradise of the nineteenth century's so-called gold standard. Twice—in the late 1920's, and again in the late 1950's—their quest seemed within reach of its goal, but in each case the illusion of success was quickly shattered by the gathering clouds of a new monetary storm. The sterling crisis of 1931 spelled the collapse of the first restoration of convertibility, and the dollar crisis of the early 1960's has finally convinced the world that the monetary order of the future cannot be found in a mere reconstruction of the past.

SOURCE: Reprinted with minor changes from Robert Triffin, "From Waterloo to Tokyo," *The Economist* (August 15, 1964). Reprinted with the permission of *The Economist*.

The Euthanasia of Gold
under the So-Called Gold Standard

The primary explanation of the success and survival of the international monetary system of the nineteenth century lay in its ability to reform itself gradually through a slow evolutionary process, of which the cumulative impact, however, was truly revolutionary. Silver coin accounted for more than a third of the world monetary stock at the beginning of the century, and for about two thirds of the additions to world money between 1815 and 1848, but declined precipitously afterward to less than 3 percent in 1913. The circulation of gold coin among the public probably declined in the first half of the century, swelled more than four times from 1848 to 1872, increased only very slightly from 1872 to 1892, and rose more rapidly again—by nearly 60 percent—from 1892 to 1913.

Such sudden and massive changes in the metallic money stock—or "commodity money"—would have played havoc with the world monetary order, if they had not been largely compensated for by parallel adaptations in the creation and acceptability of "credit money," that is, of paper currency and bank deposits. In the heyday of the so-called gold standard, paradoxically, it was in fact credit money, rather than gold or silver, which dominated the evolution of the monetary stock and fed the bulk of the monetary requirements of a growing world economy. After 1872, 95 percent of the expansion of world money was derived from bank money, as against 5 percent from silver and gold together.

High rates of economic growth were indeed reconciled with stability of exchange rates and the gold price only by the rapid growth and proper management of bank money. This could hardly have been achieved under the purely, or predominantly, metallic systems of money creation characteristic of the *previous* centuries. In truth, the nineteenth century could be far more accurately described as the century of an emerging and growing credit-money standard, and of the euthanasia of gold and silver moneys, rather than as the century of an unchanging and automatic gold standard.

The free creation of credit money by central banks of issue, in the form of currency notes, and by deposit banks, in the form of demand deposits, entailed the danger of overexpansion and bankruptcy for each issuing institution. For holders of credit money retained the legal right to convert it at will into metallic money, and they freely did so: for settlements beyond the country's borders, for wage payments and ordinary household spending, or because of diffidence about the solvency of the debtor bank. National central-banking systems gradually developed in each country and assumed growing rights and obligations to orient the creation of credit money and underwrite its ultimate convertibility into gold and foreign currencies. Central banks gradually concentrated into their own coffers more and more of the gold previously held as reserves by the deposit banks and in circulation among the public itself.

Thus the pace of total monetary expansion for all the countries adhering to the international gold standard was dependent not on the hazards of gold production alone, large as it was during the heyday of the system: gold production in the twenty-five years 1889–1913 is estimated to have nearly matched that in the previous four centuries. Monetary expansion was sustained also by this gradual shift of gold from the public and the deposit banks into the centralized reserves of national central banks.

The Aftermath of World War I

This slow evolutionary process had, by 1913, transformed out of all recognition the international bimetallic monetary system of 1815 into national credit moneys linked together by their common convertibility into gold metal. The inflationary financing of World War I and of postwar reconstruction entailed enormous and widely divergent additions to national credit money, inevitably accompanied, and followed, by a considerable reshuffling

of exchange rates. The depreciation of continental Europe's currencies was further aggravated by vast outflows of speculative
capital to the United States and Britain. Later, these capital
flows prompted a considerable overvaluation of the pound and a
parallel undervaluation of the continental currencies. Exports,
economic activity, and employment slumped into a continued depression in Britain, while booming on the continent.

The capital that had taken refuge in London began to flow
back to the continent, particularly after the recovery and subsequent stabilization of the French franc in 1926, and additional
funds moved from London to Wall Street, where the speculative
boom was by then in full swing. The British monetary authorities tried to stop the drain on their slender gold reserves by pleading with the American authorities to keep interest rates lower
than in Britain, and with the European central banks to refrain
from converting into gold or dollars the vast amounts of sterling
balances which they had to purchase from the market to prevent an appreciation of their own currencies.

The first of these two techniques soon ran counter to powerful market trends and anticyclical objectives of national policy,
both in the United States and in Britain. The second involved a
radical shift by central banks from the traditional gold standard
to the so-called gold-exchange standard, under which major gold-
convertible *national* currencies—primarily sterling and the dollar—would be accumulated by central banks as legally valid
international monetary reserves, alongside gold itself. This shift
had been tentatively recommended as one of the ways to remedy
the threatening gold shortage by various conferences. It had
been largely implemented in the 1920's on an *ad hoc,* voluntary
basis and had indeed contributed to hiding the underlying weakness of sterling in the early years after World War I.

The marathon conference of the Gold Delegation of the
League of Nations was still discussing the feasibility of firmer
agreements to organize and consolidate the new system when the
crash of a Vienna bank unleashed a new wave of speculation
throughout Europe, undermining further the highly vulnerable
position of sterling in the world markets. Britain threw in the

sponge on September 21, 1931. Sterling's inconvertibility sounded the death-knell of the system and ushered in a prolonged period of international monetary nationalism which rekindled the economic and political crisis of the 1930's, which had given signs of abating earlier in 1931.

The Aftermath of World War II

The aftermath of World War II has so far repeated, step by step, the aftermath of World War I, with the substitution of the United States for Britain as the haven for refugee capital, of the dollar for sterling as the anchor of the new gold-exchange standard, and of the international liquidity problem for the gold shortage as the recurrent theme of a frustratingly endless international monetary debate.

Fortunately, the differences are also essential. First of all, the world economy is in far better shape today than it was in 1931 and the economic and financial position of the United States far stronger than that of 1931 Britain. Secondly, the world's financial and political leaders are now keenly aware of the disastrous consequences that any repetition of the 1931 policies, or lack of policies, could entail. The latent dollar crisis of the last five years has been met by an unprecedented degree of international cooperation, and a wide array of short-term agreements among the major governments and central banks has so far shored up the new gold-exchange standard against a new collapse à la 1931.

Last, but foremost, the basic haphazardness and vulnerability of the present system of international reserve creation—and destruction—is now, for the first time, widely understood by academic economists and responsible officials alike. Who could, indeed, defend any longer a system of reserve creation under which, over the last six years (1960–1965), for instance, Russian gold sales in Western markets contributed more than two thirds of the total gold-reserve increases of the West, and under which the deficits of the two reserve-center countries fed about three fourths of the total reserve increases of other countries? How could anyone regard such a system—or rather lack of system—as a safe and rational way to regulate the increase of international reserves that must serve as the ultimate basis, particularly when currencies are convertible, for the increases in national money supplies necessary to support growing levels of production and trade in an expanding world economy? Legitimate, noninflationary reserve requirements of economic growth can hardly be defined—and met—by the algebraic additions of the monetary gold released by new production in a country threatened with civil war and by Leonid Brezhnev and Alexsei Kosygin's sales in Western markets, *minus* the erratic amounts absorbed by private gold speculators and industrial and artistic uses, *plus* the financing of variable American and British payments deficits through voluntary, or not so voluntary, accumulations of dollar and sterling IOU's by central banks, *minus* the ever possible conversions into gold metal of such IOU's accumulated over many past years.

Evolution, Revolution, or Regression?

My own long-term proposals for monetary reform, first formulated in 1959,[1] contemplate further evolutionary changes in the direction traced by the past history of world money. I shall restate them bluntly in the next chapter, before turning attention to the meandering course of the official negotiations now in process.

Before closing this introductory chapter, however, let me emphasize the relation of these proposals to past evolutionary trends:

1. They regard as inevitable in the long run a continued growth of international credit reserves alongside gold-metal reserves, just as credit money gradually supplemented, and

---

[1] In two articles of the *Banca Nazionale del Lavoro Quarterly Review*, later assembled in *Gold and the Dollar Crisis* (New Haven, Conn.: Yale University Press, 1960).

eventually replaced, gold and silver moneys in the national circulation of each country.

2. They regard as especially necessary a concerted orientation of this process, aiming to adjust the total pace of reserve growth to the noninflationary growth potential of the world economy, just as the development of national credit money in the nineteenth century imposed a similar orientation, on a national scale, under the aegis of central banks or other national monetary authorities.

3. The partial merging of national monetary sovereignties entailed by such an evolution of our international monetary system need be no larger, and could be far better gauged and understood, than that already involved today in the bewildering overlapping of IMF quotas, general arrangements to borrow, the gold-pool agreement, bilateral swaps, swap standbys, and the rest, to say nothing of the semivoluntary accumulation and retention, as international reserves, of national currencies always subject to devaluation, blocking, and inconvertibility by the unilateral decision of the debtor countries. Far greater losses of sovereignty are involved today: (a) for the creditor countries by the accumulation of dollar or sterling reserve claims, which contribute inevitably to the financing of United States or United Kingdom deficits and policies in which they have no voice and with which they may thoroughly disagree; and (b) for the debtor countries by the constant threat of sudden and massive conversions into scarce gold metal of the indebtedness piled up by them toward other central banks over the course of many years past.

4. The international lending potential that would be derived from such a system should not be used blindly for automatic lending to any and all countries in deficit, but should be earmarked to support agreed-upon policies of monetary stabilization against temporary balance-of-payments pressures, particularly in connection with capital

movements. It would thus powerfully stimulate the long-run harmonization of member countries' policies, and would help to avoid unnecessary recourse to exchange restrictions, devaluation, or deflation by the deficit countries.

5. An orderly and adequate growth of world reserves would also provide indirect support for long-term development financing, through investments in marketable obligations of international institutions, such as the World Bank.

Taken in conjunction, the credit criteria suggested above would essentially tend to recreate some of the basic features of the adjustment mechanism of the nineteenth-century gold standard. Vast amounts of private long-term lending then cushioned, for long periods of time, the current-account deficits of developing countries. Similar stabilizing capital movements could now be induced by a convincingly stable international monetary framework.

Such thoroughgoing reforms, however, are most unlikely ever to be introduced overnight, as the outcome of a grand negotiation. They will develop more gradually as the result of *ad hoc* decisions and of the more modest reforms and limping compromises to which international negotiations are usually condemned.

4

The Long-Run Evolution

of Our International

Monetary System

The negotiating constraints mentioned in the last paragraph of the preceding chapter are provisionally ignored in the present chapter in favor of a neater, bolder, but somewhat academic, outline of the long-run aims that should, in my opinion, guide and inspire future attempts at monetary reform. They will be taken into account in the later chapters reviewing the actual course of recent negotiations and indicating how the short-term agreements most urgently needed and attainable today could help pave the way for further evolutionary progress tomorrow.

Basic Features

The basic features of such an outline are taken up first, leaving various objections and alternatives for later examination.

A SINGLE RESERVE CENTER

The long-term consolidation of the international reserve system, and the adaptation of international reserve creation to the full, noninflationary growth potential of the world economy, would obviously be enormously facilitated by the adoption of a single clearing and reserve Center for national central banks. Each central bank would hold all of its monetary reserves—except for moderate, day-to-day working balances—in the form of international deposits with such a Center.

Central banks would acquire, at the start, their initial reserve deposit with the Center by transferring to it their outstanding holdings of gold and other convertible reserve assets (see the section on consolidation of outstanding currency-reserve balances, page 69 below).

CASH SETTLEMENTS

The Center would then operate as a clearing agency for all subsequent international settlements not cleared by the private exchange market itself. Three types of operations would come under this heading:

1. Direct settlements among central banks would be effected by mere bookkeeping transfers, debiting the account of the payor and crediting the account of the payee.

2. Stabilization interventions by central banks on the exchange markets involve either the purchase, or the sale, of foreign exchange by the bank concerned. The foreign currencies needed to reconstitute working balances depleted by such sales would be bought from the Center, through corresponding debits in the buying bank's reserve account. Conversely, foreign currencies—in excess of working balances—accumulated by a central bank in opposite stabilization interventions would be transferred to the Center and credited to the depositing bank's reserve account.

The reserve account of the central bank whose currency had been sold to the Center would be debited by the amount transferred. In the opposite case, when a currency is bought from the

Center, two alternative techniques could be considered. The simplest one would be for all central banks to authorize the Center to sell their currency directly against corresponding credits to their reserve account. The other would be for the Center to accumulate and maintain adequate working balances in the major currencies used in fact in such stabilization operations.

3. A third type of cash transaction would relate to the Center's purchases and sales of gold and depend very much on the future policies jointly adopted among the world's monetary authorities regarding the suspension or continuation of the support extended by them up to now to the stabilization of gold-metal prices.

Under the radical reforms envisaged above, gold could well be dispensed with as a medium of reserve accumulation, by the Center as well as by the national central banks. The essential requirement of a national currency is to be generally acceptable in payment within the country's borders. Such general acceptability can be elicited by other means than convertibility in gold metal, in one case as well as in the other, and we shall examine below (see pp. 69–70) how this could be done.

The continued guarantee of stable gold prices by the Center, or the world central banks, would then be tantamount to a decision to continue the traditional support given to gold-metal prices by the purchases of the monetary authorities. The main arguments in favor of such a policy would be:

1 . To take advantage of the continued popular illusion that gold reserves alone can constitute an effective barrier against inflation and a proper backing for the liabilities of central banks—or of the proposed Center itself;

2 . To avoid the bookkeeping losses that a demonetization of gold would almost certainly entail;

3 . To avert a sudden disruption of the economies of the major gold-producing countries.

None of these arguments is very powerful, and the latter two problems could be solved, in a different manner, on their own merits. On the other hand, the continuation of gold support prices might well require very large purchases of gold and unleash inflationary increases in world reserve assets and monetary liabilities, if the contemplated reform were to trigger large gold dishoarding by speculators. This would not be inconceivable, once people fully realized that such a reform had equipped central banks with ample means to dispense with gold altogether, and—at the very least—to rule out any probability of an increase in world gold prices in the foreseeable future.

If the decision were nevertheless adopted to support the world gold price at its present level, official interventions in the private gold market could be conducted either by the Center itself or by the central banks. In the latter case, central banks would sell to the Center—against corresponding credits to their reserve account—any gold purchased in the course of such stabilization operations; and they would buy from the Center—against corresponding debits to their account—the gold they might need to sell.

Until the U.S.S.R. and the countries associated with it decided to join the Center, any of the techniques described above would strengthen the Western world against any possible abuse of the large gold stock—and gold production—of these countries for disruptive interventions, of an economic-warfare character, in the Western gold markets.

CREDIT OPERATIONS

The major central banks, at least, will probably wish to continue to increase their reserve levels—in future years as well as in the past—in order to facilitate the maintenance of international convertibility, at stable rates of exchange, of the rising amounts of their national currency issues needed to support expanding levels of production. The mechanism of reserve creation should adjust to this fact and promote a continuous adaptation of the world's reserve pool to the demand for reserves associated with feasible rates of noninflationary growth in world trade and production.

Under the reform suggested here, all—if gold price support is abandoned—or a large portion, at least, of the necessary reserve increases would have to be derived from the progressive expansion of the Center's loan and investment portfolio. The pace of overall increases should be determined jointly, in the light of —and in such a way as to combat or moderate—discernible inflationary or deflationary pressures of a worldwide character.

Prospective surplus countries, however, will probably want to incorporate in treaty form some guarantees against inflationary abuses of the Center's lending potential, since indeed this potential would otherwise be unlimited.[1] Such a treaty might specify, for instance, a presumptive ceiling of 3 to 5 percent in any twelve-month period, on the net expansion of the Center's global assets and liabilities. Such a ceiling would not necessarily be reached in any period of time—particularly at times of inflationary pressures—but it could not, in any case, be exceeded, except by qualified voting majorities of two thirds, three fourths, or even more, of the total voting power.

Within these broad limitations, individual loan and investment operations would be designed to support mutually acceptable policies of member countries against temporary balance-of-payments pressures, thus providing a powerful stimulus for the long-run harmonization of members' policies, and the avoidance of unnecessary recourse to exchange restrictions, devaluation, or deflation by the deficit countries.

Desirable balance-of-payments disciplines upon countries following persistently inflationary policies would therefore be maintained, and indeed reinforced. No country could escape them through the automatic, but erratic and precarious, access to international borrowing enjoyed in the past by the reserve-currency countries—a type of borrowing the haphazard use and liquidation of which could unleash at any time highly disruptive

[1] Excessive lending to deficit-prone countries would merely increase *pari passu* the assets and liabilities of the Center. Subsequent drawings on their deposits by the borrowers could only reshuffle the Center's liabilities among its depositors, without producing any decline in overall liabilities. A worldwide Center would therefore be exempt from the discipline exercised upon a national central bank by national balance-of-payments deficits, in the same way as a national central bank can elude the discipline exercised upon commercial banks by losses of deposits from the more expansionary to the less expansionary banks of the system.

forces upon these countries themselves, upon the rest of the world, and upon the stability of the international gold-exchange standard.

The nature of the Center's lending operations would have to be adapted to the character of the resources used by it. Since its overall portfolio would be called upon to expand continually —although at a variable rate—over the years to come, but rarely —if ever—to be substantially contracted, some of its loans and investments might be granted in theory for extended maturities. They might even take a form similar to that of the famed British "consols," without any repayment date whatsoever, but on which interest would be paid indefinitely by the borrowers. This would make it easier to channel the world's thirst for reserves into long-term development financing of the countries most in need of such assistance.

Yet, direct long-term loans to, or investments in, the under-developed countries by the Center may well be regarded as unad-visable as well as unnecessary in practice. They would, first, have to overcome powerful taboos in the financial community whose "orthodox" canons, inspired by commercial-banking criteria, would damn any long-term assets as inappropriate backing for the short-term liabilities of a monetary institution. Second, even though its total portfolio would not be subject to the threat of sudden and massive contraction, the Center should remain able to reshuffle its loans and investments among members, in order to counteract undesirable capital movements and other short-term disturbances in the international balance-of-payments pattern. Third, long-term investments require a very different type of knowledge and expertise than those that should be relevant to stabilization interventions in the exchange market.

The bulk of the Center's assistance to long-term development financing should thus, in all probability, be channeled through —and cushioned by—intermediary institutions, specialized in such long-term lending. The Center might, for instance, distrib-ute its investment portfolio between marketable obligations of international institutions, such as the International Bank for Re-construction and Development, and other short-term or medium-term investments in the major financial centers—New York, London, Paris, Frankfurt, Amsterdam, and so on—enabling these to engage more boldly and actively in long-term lending, in the knowledge that temporary pressures on the country's reserves would be offset by a reshuffling of the Center's own investment portfolio.

Taken in conjunction with one another, the credit criteria suggested above would essentially tend to recreate some of the basic features of the adjustment mechanism of the nineteenth-century gold standard. (See above, chapter 1, pp. 13–16.) Vast amounts of private long-term lending then cushioned, for long periods of time, the current-account deficits of developing countries and made more bearable and acceptable the discipline exercised upon monetary policy by residual balance-of-payments pressures. Fifty years of monetary and economic instability and the constant threat of governmental interference in private contracts have paralyzed, or perverted, much of these private capital flows in modern times. They can be revived, in part, and redirected by official policies designed to stabilize the international framework in which they take place. They have, in addition, been supplemented by official lending, which can itself be further encouraged and better distributed as between the United States and other countries, by the international underwriting of monetary stabilization policies.

Similarly, concerted international action is necessary today to harmonize relative rates of monetary and banking expansion in such a way as to preserve long-run balance in the international pattern of payments, without unnecessary recourse to trade or exchange restrictions or exchange-rate readjustments. Market pressures, arising from deposit losses and cash settlements by the more expansionist to the less expansionist banks, usually sufficed, in the nineteenth century, to ensure such harmonization among *individual* banks—and therefore, among national banking systems—*irrespective of the existence of national political borders*. This ceased to be true as

1. Commercial banks' cash assets progressively shifted from

internationally acceptable commodity moneys—gold and/
or silver—to nationally issued credit money; *and*

2. Central banks' credit policies and monetary issues became more and more responsive to a variety of national objectives—such as price stabilization and satisfactory employment levels and growth rates—competing with, and often
overriding, their initial concern with the maintenance of
international reserve levels fully adequate to preserve full
convertibility of their own liabilities into gold or foreign exchange, at stable rates.

International consultation among responsible national monetary authorities has thus become the only effective channel for
the development of compatible and mutually supporting policies and the minimization of unnecessary recourse to internationally disruptive, contagious, and mutually defeating policy
measures. Unilateral action by the deficit countries alone to eliminate rapidly any emerging balance-of-payments disequilibria—
whether lasting or temporary—often contributes to the unnecessary adoption and spread of deflation, devaluation, and/or trade
and exchange restrictions among member countries. Concerted
action by surplus and deficit countries alike can certainly offer
far more attractive, even though often slower-acting, means to
correct such disequilibria over time, with a minimum of disruption of the national economies concerned. Conditional access to
the Center's lending resources would (1) provide an added
stimulus to such policy harmonization, and deterrent to unilateral action, (2) supplement the deficit country's ability to
finance residual, temporary deficits through the depletion of its
independent monetary reserves, and (3) discourage speculative
capital movements, which might otherwise create further, and
possibly unbearable, drains on such reserves.[2]

---

[2] Complementary—and partly alternative—measures aiming at a better adaptation of the world reserve pool itself to noninflationary growth requirements of
the world economy are amply discussed in other chapters of this volume.

CONSOLIDATION OF OUTSTANDING CURRENCY-RESERVE BALANCES

The transition from the old system to the new would, of course, involve a once-and-for-all type of credit operations determined by the treaty itself, that is, the transfer to the Center of the large currency-reserve balances now held by member countries.

The Center would, as a result, initiate its operations with large credit claims on the United States and the United Kingdom, inherited from many years of functioning of the gold-exchange standard. There would be no reason to liquidate systematically such investments, long incorporated into the international reserve system itself. Provisions for their amortization—through equivalent debits to the debtor's reserve account—should be limited in the following manner:

1. Voluntary amortization, at the request of the debtor;

2. Compensatory amortization up to the amounts of current reserve increases bringing their overall level above some agreed-upon—"normal" (?)—ratio to the country's imports;

3. An optional right for the Center to request additional amortization by no more than x percent—5 percent, for example—of the country's outstanding debt balance (if regarded as necessary); such option, however, to be exercised only when deemed necessary to meet other countries' legitimate requests for assistance without expanding the global loan and investment portfolio of the Center, and when compatible with the preservation of an adequate reserve level and the pursuit of internationally acceptable policies by the debtor.

INTERNATIONAL GUARANTEES

All the claims and debts of the Center should obviously carry adequate guarantees against unilateral inconvertibility, or exchange-devaluation decisions, or default by the debtors. Some common unit of account, adapted from the EPU unit of account, could be used for that purpose in all Center transactions and embody in effect an exchange guarantee in terms of whichever currency remains most stable in the future. Alternatively, this exchange guarantee could be expressed in terms of a weighted average of the major currencies used in world trade and payments.

Guarantees against default could be provided in two ways:

1. Through a commitment of all members to channel, as far as possible, through the defaulting country's account with the Center, all payments due to it until the default is made up;

2. Through a geographical distribution of the Center's gold assets, approximating, on a pro rata basis, the pattern of the Center's deposit liabilities to its members.

Such guarantees would indeed erect stronger safeguards against defaults than any ever devised in past international lending operations.

Other Issues, Objections, and Alternatives

Serious objections have been raised against the proposals described above, particularly by those enamoured with "national sovereignty" and "flexible exchange rates."

SURRENDERS OF NATIONAL SOVEREIGNTY?

Proposals such as these are lightly shrugged off in many circles as involving revolutionary surrenders of national sovereignty to a worldwide "superbank," incapable in fact of discharging its responsibilities without the full backing of a supranational world government.

The money created by a super-bank would be the most high powered ever generated by a man-made institution, yet it would have no supporting super-government to make good on its debts or claims . . . Simply to establish the super-bank would require all countries of the world to give up their present reserves and accept instead the fiat issue of a super-authority existing without a super-state.[3]

These emotional slogans bear little or no relation to the concrete content of the long-term proposals developed above. They are even less relevant to the more modest suggestions for short- or medium-term negotiations that will be outlined in the following section of this study, and which would merely streamline and rationalize the technical provisions endowing the International Monetary Fund with whatever level of lending capacity is deemed appropriate by its members and is now derived from equivalent, but far more rigid, arbitrary and cumbersome capital subscriptions and other national commitments (such as those embodied in the so-called General Arrangements to Borrow).

Reserve holders would retain, under the plan, far more control over the size and use of future accretions to world credit reserves than they have had—or now have—over the size and use of the IOU's dropped by the reserve-currency centers into the world's reserve pool. They would, it is true, renounce their present right to sudden and massive cashing of their credit reserves into gold metal, but they well know that such a right has already become largely theoretical and could not be exercised in fact on a large scale without bringing to an end the effective convertibility of the currencies involved and without causing the collapse of the international gold-exchange standard itself.

Prospective borrowers, on the other hand, would in no way be forced to accept the advice—and the investments—offered them by the Center. They could refuse both, if they wish, particularly as the Center could not invest in their market without obtaining from the national authorities in charge the exchange

[3] Robert V. Roosa, "Assuring the Free World's Liquidity," *Business Review Supplement,* Federal Reserve Bank of Philadelphia (September, 1962), p. 8. More concrete objections are developed in the following paragraphs of the text, which quote the conflicts and disturbances that might arise from sudden shifts by individual countries from international deposits to national currency holdings or to gold metal. This might better be formulated, however, as a valid stricture on the present gold-exchange standard than as a criticism of proposals specifically designed to protect the international monetary system against such unnecessary sources of disturbance. Anyway, Mr. Roosa now also advocates a man-made international reserve asset.

guarantees described under the section "International Guarantees" above.

Present reserve borrowers, moreover, would regain—through the transfer to the Center of their outstanding indebtedness to central banks—a degree of control over future monetary policies strongly handicapped today by the volatile character of this indebtedness.

Neither would the joint consultations and decisions relating to the Center's investments be revolutionary in character nor involve necessarily the setting up of supranational institutions or voting rules. The IMF and the EPU, for instance, have long functioned essentially along the lines suggested here without raising any objection to their supranational character.

Finally, the Center could hardly be described as a world central bank, since its reserve liabilities would circulate only among the national central banks themselves, and these would retain full control over, and responsibility for, their currency issues, each within its own national territory. One consequence of this is that exchange readjustments could in no way be ruled out, and would indeed prove imperative at times for countries that failed to harmonize their monetary policies with those prevalent in the world community.

This raises a broad question that cannot be adequately explored within the confines of the present paper, that is, the proper scope of institutional commitments to exchange-rate stability.

STABLE VERSUS FLUCTUATING RATES

This question is usually discussed in abstract terms, as if the same solution were always advisable for all countries and at all times. I would prefer to answer it in terms very similar to those given to it in a recent paper of Ronald I. McKinnon.[4]

I have myself long expressed a preference for stable exchange rates, subject to readjustments only in the case of obvious failure

[4] "Optimum World Monetary Arrangements and the Dual Currency System," *Banca Nazionale del Lavoro Quarterly Review* (December, 1963), pp. 366–396. See also a brief communication on "Optimum Currency Areas," *The American Economic Review* (September, 1963), pp. 717–725.

to preserve adequate cost competitiveness for long-run equilibrium in the country's balance of payments at optimum levels of employment, economic growth, and trade and exchange liberalization. This preference was based on three main arguments:[5]

1. Stable exchange rates tend to spread and even out among the trading countries the inflationary and deflationary gaps arising from differential rates of national monetary and financial expansion. Balance-of-payments disequilibria and changes in monetary reserves provide, under this system, an alternative outlet to the development of domestic pressures—upward in the more expansionist countries, and downward in the less expansionist ones—upon prices and employment, and do indeed bear a far closer relationship to differential rates of monetary expansion than to differential changes in national price and cost levels.[6] The latter tend in fact to be kept roughly in line with one another through the impact of competition in internationally traded goods—and particularly by export competition in third markets—as long as domestic policies can be readjusted in time to avoid devaluation or trade and exchange restrictions, isolating national price levels from one another.

Freely floating rates—à la Friedman—would "bottle up" within each country's borders the inflationary or deflationary pressures arising from every expansionist or contractionist error in domestic policies. Exchange-rate fluctuations would absorb the full brunt of the disequilibria formerly cushioned by reserve gains or losses and help preserve competitiveness in each country's current-account transactions; but they would also lift the barrier previously erected by stable exchange rates against divergent movements in national price and cost levels.

The upward flexibility of wage rates would, moreover, tend to sanction with permanent and irreversible wage increases any

[5] See Robert Triffin, *Gold and the Dollar Crisis* (New Haven, Conn.: Yale University Press, 1960), pp. 82–86.

[6] See Robert Triffin and Herbert G. Grubel, "The Adjustment Mechanism to Differential Rates of Monetary Expansion Among the Countries of the European Economic Community," *Review of Economics and Statistics* (November, 1962), pp. 486–491; reprinted in *The World Money Maze: National Currencies in International Payments* (New Haven, Conn.: Yale University Press, 1966), pp. 29–38.

inflationary mistakes or mishaps in monetary and credit policies, and any consequent increases in foreign-exchange rates, import costs, and consumers' prices; while deflationary errors would be unlikely to result in parallel, and offsetting, downward wage adjustments in a modern economy. Freely floating rates could hardly fail, therefore, to introduce a permanent bias toward currency depreciation—at least in terms of goods, if all countries adopted the system—and to elicit from Friedman's highly farsighted speculators one-way flights from the national currency into equities, real assets, gold, and/or foreign exchange, rather than alternating, and "stabilizing" capital inflows and outflows. Such destabilizing capital movements might, it is true, still be dubbed "equilibrating," but merely in the sense of accelerating the adjustment of exchange rates to price and cost disparities fostered by the system itself, and which might have been avoided under a system of stable exchange rates.

2. "Managed" floating rates—à la Meade—are too often advocated as though each country could determine by itself a desired rate in respect to all other countries. Exchange rates, however, express a relation between *several* currencies. Will the sterling-dollar rate, for instance, be abandoned by the United States to British management, or by the United Kingdom to United States management? And what will happen if the countries involved take a different view of the "desirable" rate between their currencies? (Meade himself is, of course, perfectly logical in his proposal, and recognizes that it involves the surrender of such management, by all countries, to an *International* Equalization Account.)

3. Finally, I doubt whether floating rates can really provide, in the long run, a viable bridge between persistently divergent national monetary policies. They are far more likely to be a form of escapism, for which other and better methods could be substituted in the case of merely temporary lapses from responsible monetary management, and which would merely end in currency collapse in the case of protracted inflationary developments.

The spectacular growth and success of European monetary

cooperation and policy harmonization since World War II seems to me to demonstrate the feasibility of an alternative path, far more deserving of support than the advocacy of exchange-rate-flexibility palliatives to monetary nationalism.

Yet, I would agree that these arguments are particularly applicable to the case of exchange relations between relatively small, highly open and competitive economies, capable of developing a satisfactory—and, in this case, highly desirable—degree of monetary cooperation and policy harmonization with one another. They are far less applicable to the exchange relations between larger countries, or groups of countries, which, because their external transactions are dwarfed by the size of their internal markets, are far better able to conduct effective monetary policies on their own and are therefore far less interested and willing to subordinate their freedom of action to international consultation and effective policy harmonization.

Even in this case, however, the elimination of national currencies as an international reserve medium would remain a necessary prerequisite for the successful implementation and functioning of exchange-rate flexibility, particularly in the case of the present reserve-center countries.

WHETHER AND WHEN?

So-called realists will merely shrug their shoulders at the above proposals and dismiss them with the simple word: "Utopia!" They will prefer to "build directly upon the existing payments procedures to which governments and individuals are already well accustomed." [7] In the words of Erich Fromm, "it is, indeed, one of the irrationalities of human nature that we are prone to seek for easier, short-term solutions because we are afraid of the difficulties of the fundamental and real solutions. But in individual as in social life, it is the logic of facts that determines reality, not the logic of wishful thinking." [8]

This is why I have little doubt about the inevitability of a

[7] Robert V. Roosa, "Assuring the Free World's Liquidity," p. 12.
[8] Erich Fromm, *May Man Prevail?* (New York: Anchor Books, 1961), pp. 207–208.

continued evolution of our international monetary institutions
in a direction so clearly charted by the historical development
of *national* monetary systems in every country of the world,
and by similar trends already perceptible in the changing structure of the *international* reserve system itself over the last half
century.

In every country, "commodity money" has been gradually
displaced by "credit money" (see Tables 1.2 and 1.3 at the end
of Chapter 1, above). Credit money remained at first unorganized,
and its creation—or destruction—abandoned to the uncoordinated decisions and policies of multiple issue and deposit banks.
The instability of such a system prompted the development of
national central banks. These did not replace and eliminate
previous institutions, but assumed initially centralized clearing
and reserve functions, out of which further instruments for
policy coordination and orientation of bank credit and monetary
expansion developed gradually over the years. As in the case of
other human institutions, this evolution was rarely blueprinted
in advance through conscious planning. It came, in most cases, as
the unforeseen consequence of "short-term" expedients, adopted
to meet pressing problems and crises, but which then developed
a life of their own through the internal logic of institutional
adaptation to man's changing environment.

Speaking of the development of the gold standard itself,
Jacques Mertens noted that:

> Most of those interventions do not flow from any clearly
> planned monetary policy and objectives. In general, the authorities
> intervene only in case of difficulties, during periods of monetary
> troubles. Time is then of the essence, and action is most often
> limited to partial and temporary measures. . . . What emerges
> are compromise solutions along the path of least resistance, whose
> merit in the eyes of the administrators is that they do not com-
> mit them in the future, but leave them a free hand to determine
> later final decisions whose timing is always postponed. It has cer-
> tainly been one of the most tenacious illusions of the executive
> power to believe that by postponing decisions, by cumulating
> temporary expedients and half-measures, it retained its freedom of

action. Have we not seen, on the contrary, that repeatedly and without wishing it, administrations have put their finger in the cog and have found themselves dragged on, against their will, toward unexpected results by measures which they considered as totally secondary or purely temporary? [9]

The displacement of "commodity money" by "credit money," in national monetary systems, finds an exact parallel in the incipient, but fast growing, displacement of "commodity reserves" by "credit reserves," in the international field. The proportion of credit reserves (foreign exchange and IMF claims) to total reserves has grown, for countries other than the reserve centers themselves, from little over 20 percent in 1913, as in 1937, to more than 50 percent in 1966.

The bulk of these credit reserves is still held in national reserve currencies, but the proportions of these latter to total reserves exhibit, in spite of the huge United States and United Kingdom deficits which feed them, a pronounced declining trend: from 56 percent in 1949 down to 40 percent at the end of 1966. On the other hand, the share of reserve claims on the IMF in the gross reserves of the nonreserve-center countries has risen sharply, over the same period, from 1 percent only to 11 percent.

This contrasting evolution corresponds exactly to the long-term evolution contemplated in this chapter, that is, the substitution of *international* claims for *national*—primarily dollar and sterling—claims in the world reserve system. The main question facing us today is not whether this evolution will continue over the sweep of history, but whether the international agreements necessary to that effect will be negotiated in time to avert further crises, such as that which swept away nearly overnight the "national currencies" component of the 1931 international reserves and brought about a protracted collapse of the international monetary system.

[9] Jacques E. Martens, *La naissance et le développement de l'étalon-or, 1696–1922* (Louvain and Paris, 1944), pp. 356–357.

Three Major Issues:
Proper Use, Amount, and
Composition of Reserves

Three separate, but closely related, problems dominate the debate on international monetary reform.

The first two correspond to the two sections of Chapter 1 of this volume. The first concerns the mutual adjustment of national policies to one another in an increasingly interdependent world, and the second the factors determining the creation—or destruction—of the international pool of monetary reserves necessary to support optimum rates of expansion in world trade and production. The third is really a special case of the second, but deserves separate consideration. It relates to the vulnerability imparted to the system by the concurrent use of three distinct types of reserve assets, and particularly by the exposure of the reserve currencies to sudden and massive conversions of their excessive reserve indebtedness into scarce gold metal.

The Mutual Adjustment of National Policies

I have dwelled at length, in the first part of this volume, on the implications of the shift from laissez faire to state interventions in all aspects of economic life, and particularly in the field of money creation. The issue and control of fiduciary money has become one of the most jealously guarded privileges of national sovereignty. These national fiduciary moneys, however, circulate only within each country's borders and have to be converted into one another for the settlement of all transactions crossing such borders. National monetary authorities are ultimately charged with the responsibility of assuring such conversions of their own currency into foreign currencies, or of foreign currencies into their own, to satisfy the net demand of all other transactors not cleared by the market itself.

Whenever they sell their domestic currency against foreign currencies, they use in fact their money-creating power to lend to the foreign countries whose currency they accumulate as reserves. This may have a welcome expansionary, or an unwelcome inflationary, effect upon their own economy. On the other hand, the sale of foreign currencies, previously accumulated as reserves, has the opposite effects. It cancels the credit previously extended to foreigners and mops up an equivalent amount of domestic money supply.

Let us analyze separately these internal and external impacts of central banks' interventions on the exchange market.

INTERNAL IMPACT

The internal impact of these operations is the very core of the classical mechanism of balance-of-payments adjustment. The expansionist impact of reserve accumulation tends to raise domestic demand and, when full employment is approached, domestic price and cost levels, thus diverting more and more of the expanded domestic demand into purchases both of foreign goods and of exportable home-produced goods. Imports will rise, exports will fall, and the overall "monetary surplus," which had triggered reserve accumulation, will tend to disappear. The deflationary, or disinflationary, impact of reserve losses, on the other hand, will have an opposite impact on domestic demand, price and cost levels, exports and imports and will tend to eliminate the "monetary deficit" responsible for the loss of reserves. The downward rigidity of wages, however, is likely to throw much of this adjustment burden on employment rather than on cost levels.

The domestic impact of interest-rate changes will accelerate these readjustments. The additions to money supply associated with foreign-exchange absorption by the central banks would tend to depress interest rates and further encourage investment demand, while the contraction of money supply associated with reserve losses would tend to raise interest rates and slow down investment demand. These effects would thus also work toward a return to balance-of-payments equilibrium, although they would be gradually counteracted by the feedback of the readjusting changes on investment demand.

Changes in interest rates, however, may also elicit *international* capital movements accelerating the readjustment of the country's overall "monetary balance," but drying up also, by the same token, the very source of the "current-account" readjustments described above.

All these monetary impacts of central bank reserve fluctuations bear, of course, primarily on the cash holdings of other banks and have a multiplied effect on their lending potential and thus, ultimately, upon the money stock in the hands of the public.[1]

The monetary authorities may speed up this readjustment process even further, or, on the contrary, offset it partly or wholly, through the conduct of their own credit policies and their advice to the fiscal authorities. The reserve-losing and

[1] Neglect of this factor vitiates, to my mind, much of Ragnar Nurkse's analysis of the "rules of the game" and of their frustration through "neutralization," in Chapter IV of his *International Currency Experience* (League of Nations, 1944).

reserve-gaining countries, however, find themselves in a very different position in this respect.

The first will often be tempted, or forced by political pressures, to try to offset the deflationary impact of their reserve losses upon the economy. This, however, will frustrate the adjustment mechanism described above and lead to a gradual depletion of their reserve stock, forcing them in the end to abandon these "neutralization" policies or to resort to restrictions or depreciation to arrest the drain of their reserves.

The authorities of the surplus countries may be equally concerned about the inflationary impact of their reserve gains, once they have reached full employment. The effective implementation of neutralization policies by them, however, will often prove as difficult and unpalatable politically, as it is easy in the case of the deficit countries. If they succeed, nevertheless, in carrying out such policies, continued reserve gains will not bump against any hard financial ceiling, such as the one imposed by the depletion of reserves upon the neutralization policies of the deficit countries. The actual burden of readjustment policies will be shifted, to that extent, from the surplus countries to the deficit countries, in highly asymmetrical fashion, and the imbalance between surplus and deficit countries finally eliminated only when the latter countries have been forced, willy-nilly, to eliminate their deficits.

This asymmetry has long been denounced by the economists as reflecting a "deflationary bias" in the gold-standard mechanism, but the stricture would apply equally to most of the alternative systems of international settlements that could be proposed with any realistic chance of being acceptable to prospective surplus countries. This deflationary *financial* bias, moreover, is often accompanied in practice by the opposite inflationary *political* bias noted in the preceding paragraph. Unfortunately, these two biases do not necessarily offset each other. As in the old fable "The Oyster and the Litigants," there is a third solution to the dilemma: the political inflationary bias may prevail and the financial deflationary bias be eluded through devaluation or restrictions. History strongly suggests that the main bias of the international monetary system of the last half century has been a bias toward import or exchange restrictions and currency depreciation.

These considerations hardly argue for a preservation, or even a strengthening, of the *present* adjustment mechanism. My own suggestions in this respect will be developed later (see pp. 139–143), after taking into account the close interrelationship of this problem with that of reserve creation, discussed in the next section of this chapter.[2]

Before we leave the present topic, however, another and even more glaring asymmetry of the present gold-exchange standard deserves a few words of comment. This relates to the external impact of a country's reserve gains or losses upon the economy of the other countries, and of the special problems arising in that respect from the use of *national* currencies as *international* reserves.[3]

EXTERNAL IMPACT

One might be tempted to view "monetary surpluses" and "monetary deficits,"—gains and losses of reserves by the monetary authorities—as two sides of the same coin, that is, of the imbalance between the surplus countries and the deficit countries. If this were so, the above analysis (see discussion under "Internal Impact") could be applied equally to either side of the coin, and the readjustment "burden" would be shared—even though probably unequally—between both groups of countries. This is not so, however, for several reasons.

Under a pure gold standard, the sum of the monetary sur-

[2] See also my paper "The Balance-of-Payments Seesaw" and other papers on the same topic in William Fellner, Fritz Machlup, Robert Triffin, and eleven others, *Maintaining and Restoring Balance in International Payments* (Princeton, N.J.: Princeton University Press, 1966).

[3] The proponents of flexible exchange rates may rightly deplore the lack of attention paid here to this ingenious way out of many of the difficulties raised above. My only defense is that I have said most of what I have to say on that subject on pp. 72–75 above, and that flexible exchange rates have so far been declared out of bounds—rightly or wrongly—in all official negotiations concerning international monetary reform.

pluses is larger than the sum of the monetary deficits by the excess of new gold production over current gold absorption by private channels (the arts, industry, hoarding, and speculation). Increases in the world stock of monetary gold are offset by the digging of new gold out of the earth without any reserve losses in the gold-mining countries. As long as central banks continue to stabilize the price of gold in terms of their national currencies through unlimited sales or redemptions of the latter against the first, at a fixed price, changes in the world reserve pool will be determined by the hazards of gold production and private gold purchases,[4] rather than by any rational criteria related to reserve needs.

At the opposite extreme of the gold standard, we could conceive of a *"universal national-currencies standard"* under which all balance-of-payments disequilibria would be settled through the unlimited acceptance of the deficit countries' currencies as international reserves by the surplus countries. In this case, all imbalances would be assured of unlimited financing, through the automatic lending commitment assumed by the surplus countries. The main burden of readjustment would probably fall upon the latter, since the reluctance to lend would probably be greater than the reluctance to borrow, in the absence of any specific repayment obligation other than that deriving from a reversal in the underlying transactions. The surplus countries could limit their lending and real transfers of goods and services only through reducing their surpluses themselves, for example, by welcoming—or even accelerating—the inflationary impact of their surpluses on domestic price and cost levels, restricting or taxing exports, subsidizing imports, and so on. Measures designed to stimulate private capital exports would also, of course, reduce the forced lending of their central banks, but merely by substituting one form of lending for another.

[4] The unavailability of gold-reserves and gold-production statistics for the communist countries forces us to exclude them from consideration and to introduce instead as a separate factor the net sales of gold by communist countries in the noncommunist countries.

These implications of such a system explain why it has never been adopted in the past and is most unlikely ever to be adopted in the future. Prospective creditors will find it much simpler never to assume the revolutionary commitment to automatic lending that constitutes the core of the system and that would in effect "internationalize" the national money-creating power of the deficit countries, without giving any voice to the lenders— and suppliers of "real" resources—over the management of this internationalized money-creating power.

Yet, the hybrid gold-exchange standard of the last half century incorporates some of the features of the system described above. Insofar as the surplus countries do in fact accumulate their reserve gains in the form of national currencies, they do finance automatically the deficits of the countries whose currency they accumulate. The settlement of these deficits involves, to that extent, no drain of gross reserves and therefore enables the reserve center countries to neutralize, through compensatory internal credit policies, the deflationary impact of their deficits, thus removing the kingpin of the classical mechanism of adjustment as far as they are concerned and shifting the adjustment burden to the rest of the world.

The main differences with the theoretical "universal national-currencies standard" described above are as follows:

1. The gold-exchange standard initially grew up, in the nineteenth century, within a limited group of countries, closely dependent, politically and/or financially, on a major power and financial center, such as Great Britain. The dependent countries accepted to accumulate and hold as monetary reserves the currency of the center country, but the center country did not accept in settlement the national currencies of the other members of the group. The latter, moreover, were prospective debtors rather than creditors on current account. Their "overall monetary surpluses" were primarily fed by borrowings from the center country and were unlikely to rise beyond moderate amounts regarded as desirable by the lenders as well as by the borrowers.

2. The extension of the system in the 1920's and—within the sterling area—in the 1930's was largely explainable by similar

considerations.[5] A major difference, however, was to have ominous consequences for the stability of the system: The main traditional center country, Britain, was no longer in a strong balance-of-payments position, neither on current nor on capital account, and was unable to weather the large-scale conversion of its IOU's into gold metal, which this weakened position could trigger at any time.

3. The renewed growth of sterling reserves during World War II was largely limited to politically dependent countries and areas, which had little choice in the matter.

4. The postwar growth of dollar reserves resembles the early phases of the sterling standard in that it was—and still is—supported by considerable strength in the United States balance-of-payments position on current account and by a high degree of financial dependency vis-à-vis the New York market and United States official loans and grants. Well over half of official dollar balances are still currently held by countries such as Great Britain, Canada, Japan, the Latin American republics, and other countries that are heavy borrowers here and beneficiaries of our economic and military aid programs. Of the $8.2 billion of official dollar liabilities (including nonmarketable bonds and notes) to Western European countries reported as of June, 1966, well over half is probably held by the United Kingdom, Germany, Italy, Spain, and other countries whose financial, economic, political, and military links to us are particularly strong and valued. Other countries, such as France, the Netherlands, and Belgium, also held willingly large dollar reserves in the Marshall Plan days, but now hold—as Switzerland always did—little more than minimum working balances in dollars.

5. Last but not least, the major differences between the present gold-exchange standard and the "universal national-currencies standard" are that (a) only one currency, the United States dollar, is nearly *universally* accepted, to any substantial extent, as a reserve currency; and, most of all, that (b) the holders of dollar reserves have never accepted any binding obligation to

[5] These included the financial dependency associated, but on a less durable basis, with the negotiation of "stabilization loans."

accumulate them, nor even to retain them in the future. They are free, at any time, to insist on gold settlement of their past, as well as of their current, dollar accumulation.

This last feature is indeed crucial, not only to the acceptability of the system but also to its inherent vulnerability and instability.

As brilliantly sketched by Professor Mundell, in recent testimony before the Joint Economic Committee of Congress,

> *the outer countries peg their currencies (directly or indirectly) to the inner country's currency (the dollar) and thus act as residual purchasers or sellers of dollars, while the inner country (the U.S.) pegs the dollar to the ultimate asset (gold), and thus acts as the residual buyer or seller of gold. This means that the size of the U.S. deficit determines the increase in reserves of the rest of the world, while its composition [the ways—primarily gold or dollars— in which the U.S. deficit is settled] determines the change in reserves of the U.S., given the rate of increase of monetary gold holdings in the world.*[6]

This "composition" is, in turn, freely determined by the other countries under the rules of the gold-exchange standard. None of them can protect themselves from the inflationary or deflationary pressures that fluctuations in the United States' balance of payments may unleash upon them as a group. But their *combined* choices as to whether to accumulate further dollar holdings, or at the other extreme liquidate previously accumulated dollars, will have a strong, and ultimately determining, influence on the ability of the United States to sustain further deficits—although not to sustain persistent surpluses— in its balance of payments without resorting to controls or devaluation destructive of the system itself.

These reactions of the outer countries, however, are far from coordinated, and are therefore subject to considerable

[6] *New Approach to United States International Economic Policy,* Hearings before the Subcommittee on International Exchange and Payments of the Joint Economic Committee of Congress, September 9, 1966, p. 5.

frustration for any one of them,[7] as well as to generalized waves of confidence or diffidence in the future convertibility and stability of the dollar. This makes the position of the center country highly precarious in the long run. It can, in the early phases of the popularity of its currency as a reserve instrument, finance much larger and more persistent deficits than it would be able to incur otherwise. If, however, the center country uses its leeway in this manner, the time is bound to come when other countries will shift from dollar hoarding to dollar dishoarding, either because of increasing doubts about the ultimate redeemability of their dollars at the existing gold price, or because of their desire to restrain the external inflationary impact of persistent United States deficits on their own economy, or for both of these reasons. When this happens, the United States may experience considerable and unsustainable gold losses and deflationary pressures even at times of overall equilibrium in its balance of payments, whether measured à la Lederer or even à la Bernstein (its losses of gold assets being offset by an equivalent decline in its reserve liabilities).[8]

On the other hand, if the United States restores full balance in its external transactions, it will cease to feed a world reserve pool that has become excessively dependent on the creation and acceptability of further dollar IOU's as reserves for other central banks.

In either case, the use of a national currency as a prime feeder of reserve assets for the rest of the world is bound to introduce a highly erratic and unpredictable factor both in the

[7] The option of some countries to accumulate their reserves in gold rather than dollars, for instance, does not protect them against the inflationary impact of their surpluses as long as those continue to be fed by United States deficits financed by other countries' continued dollar accumulation.

[8] Thus foreign accumulation of our dollar IOU's as reserves financed more than half of our net reserve deficits over the five years 1960–1964 ($5.9 billion out of $11.0 billion). In the first nine months of 1966, however, reserve *surpluses* of about $500 million were accompanied by a *decline* of about $575 million in our gross reserves (of which $709 million gold losses), as a result of large-scale liquidation (close to $1100 million) by foreign central banks of dollar balances previously accumulated by them.

much vaunted mechanism of balance-of-payments adjustment
and in the actual pace of growth—or contraction—of the world
reserve pool.

These observations highlight the close interdependence between the adjustment mechanism and the other two issues still
to be reviewed in this chapter.

The Creation of World Reserves

The main achievement of the current debate on international
monetary reform has been the unanimous recognition, by all
participants, of the failure of the present gold-exchange standard
to provide a satisfactory adjustment of reserve growth to reserve
needs in an expanding world economy.

RESERVE REQUIREMENTS IN AN EXPANDING WORLD ECONOMY

The demand for money is determined by the aggregate amount
of the "cash balances," or "working balances," that firms and
households find convenient to maintain, in a highly liquid form,
in view of the different—and unpredictable—timing of their
receipts and expenditures. It is supplied today by more than a
hundred national banking systems, operating in each country
under the general guidance and responsibility of national monetary authorities.

International monetary reserves are essentially the cash, or
working, balances accumulated by these national monetary authorities in order to bridge the gaps between the foreign expenditures and receipts of each country's residents and to avoid
unwanted fluctuations in exchange rates between the national
currency of which they are in charge and foreign currencies.
Whenever the overall receipts, on current and capital account,
of the country's residents exceed their payments abroad, the
monetary authorities have to sell additional amounts of their
national currency to the market, in order to prevent an appreciation of its exchange rate, and to accept in exchange either gold
or foreign currencies. In the opposite case—of an excess of pay-

ments over receipts—they must redeem in gold or foreign exchange the overflow of their national currency on the market in order to prevent a depreciation of the country's exchange rate. International monetary reserves are built up in the first case, and drawn upon in the second, in order to preserve exchange-rate stability. Undesirable or unsustainable (downward) movements in a country's exchange reserves are one of the factors that induce changes in the country's policies in order to correct the undesired consequences of an excessive rate of accumulation of monetary reserves—that is, of inflationary pressures on the domestic economy—or of an excessive rate of depletion—that is, of internal deflationary pressures, and ultimately the inability of the monetary authorities to provide the market with foreign exchange needed to avoid exchange depreciation or restrictions.

These considerations do not lend themselves to any scientific determination of an "ideal" level of reserves, either for an individual country or for the world at large. There is certainly a very wide range of actual reserve levels that might be regarded as satisfactory, or acceptable, by the monetary authorities and that would not induce them to modify their policies in such a way as to sacrifice other and more fundamental policy goals, such as desirable rates of employment and economic growth, price stability, and so on.

Percentage ratios of reserves to imports are most often used as a rough criterion of reserve adequacy, but should be usefully supplemented by ratios of reserves to money supply, or even to the sight liabilities of the monetary authorities. All such ratios, however, will exhibit wide variations from one country to another, reflecting primarily basic differences in their economic and financial structure, and over time for the same country, reflecting primarily differences in cyclical and other factors in economic and financial developments.

These variations in reserve ratios are summarized in the first four columns of Table 5.1 and are presented in greater detail in Table 2, p. 13, of the *1966 Annual Report* of the IMF. A large, and relatively "closed," economy like that of the United States should normally exhibit a high ratio of reserves to imports, but

Table 5.1　Gross Monetary Reserves, Imports and Money Supply, 1949–1964

| | PERCENTAGE RATIO OF RESERVES TO | | | | AVERAGE YEARLY GROWTH RATES 1950–1964 | | |
| | Imports | | Money Supply | | Re-serves | Im-ports | Money Supply |
	1949	1964	1949	1964			
I. Reserve centers	173	52	21	10	−2.9	6.1	2.7
United States	345	82	24	10	−3.0	5.5	2.7
United Kingdom	21	15	8	7	1.9	4.0	2.7
II. All other countries	41	40			7.1	7.3	
A. European Community	26	49	14	28	14.7	10.0	9.8
France	18	66	7	17	16.5	8.0	10.1
Germany	9	54	6	47	28.0	13.3	11.3
Italy	39	53	17	19	13.1	10.9	11.9
Netherlands	24	33	23	55	11.9	9.4	5.5
Belgium	54	37	31	36	5.5	8.3	4.4
B. Other "Group of Ten"	58	39	32	24	6.8	9.5	9.7
Sweden	23	25	22	29	8.9	8.3	6.7
Switzerland	192	86	66	48	4.2	9.9	6.4
Canada	42	38	27	37	6.0	6.6	4.0
Japan	25	25	9	8	15.7	15.6	16.8
C. Other developed areas	39	42			7.0	6.5	
D. Less developed areas	47	29			1.2	4.5	
III. World	77	43			2.8	6.9	
IV. World outside United States	38	37			6.8	6.9	

SOURCES AND NOTES:

1. All above ratios are derived from gross reserves, imports and money supply estimates published by *International Financial Statistics*, and uniformly expressed or recalculated in terms of United States dollars.

2. They probably underestimate the reserve ratios—but not the yearly growth rates—of the less-developed areas, owing to the fact that global import estimates for these areas as a whole include imports of countries and territories for which reserves are not reported or are held by other countries. The *1966 Annual Report* of the IMF (p. 13) gives much higher estimates of the ratio of reserves to imports for the less-developed countries: 64 percent, for instance, in 1951 and 40 percent for 1964.

a low ratio of reserves to money supply, while the opposite would be true for a smaller and highly "open" economy like that of the Netherlands. Poorer countries, with a less diversified economy and balance-of-payments structure may "need" larger reserves than richer and more diversified economies, but are less able to "afford" them, since reserve accumulation competes with more urgent expenditures for consumption and investment. Some, at least, of the richer countries may need high reserve levels for another reason: the greater vulnerability of a more liquid financial structure to sudden and massive changes in international capital flows.[9] In any case, the richer countries are better able to accumulate reserves and inclined to do so for political, as well as strictly economic, motives. High reserve levels give them more discretion in their economic policies by making them less dependent on foreign borrowings to finance temporary deficits in their balance of payments.

(These observations bring out again the similarity between a country's reserves and the cash balances of an individual. Reserves, just as cash balances, are—at least within a very wide range—a luxury good whose normal holdings rise more than proportionately to income.)

The low reserve levels of Britain and the Scandinavian countries reflect also a long historical tradition, possibly explainable in part by the ease with which these countries could slow down capital exports and induce capital imports and repatriation in times of need. (This may no longer be as true for Britain as in former days, and the combination of low reserve levels with excessive short-term foreign indebtedness is certainly a major factor of weakness for the British economy today.)

Reserves should, moreover, exhibit substantial variations over time if they are to serve their very purpose, that is, to cushion temporary fluctuations in balances of payments. Wider and/or persistent variations, however, are an indication of un-

---

[9] This factor probably plays a large role in the explanation of the traditionally high reserve levels of Switzerland, whose neutrality in the last two world wars has attracted larger amounts of refugee capital and short-term funds than could be profitably and safely used for domestic expansion.

wanted disturbances whose causes may be traced to national policy mishaps, but also sometimes to the system of reserve creation itself.

The persistent and spectacular postwar decline in United States reserves and increase in the reserves of most continental European countries were welcome at first as a desirable readjustment of the abnormal pattern of reserve distribution inherited from the war and its immediate aftermath. Their persistence in more recent years, however, is now universally criticized as a sign of improper adjustment policies on the part of some, or all, of the countries concerned.

On the other hand, the sharp drop of gross reserves for the world as a whole—from 77 percent of world imports in 1949 to 37 percent in 1966—must obviously be ascribed to the mechanism of reserve creation rather than to the policies of any country or group of countries. Even more striking is the fact that this proportion would have fallen more dramatically, from 72 percent to only 29 percent, if the United States had kept itself in balance and refrained from feeding the world reserve pool with an ever-growing mass of dollar IOU's.

In view of the above complexities, desirable *rates of increase* in monetary reserves may be both easier to define and more important operationally than absolute levels at any given point in time (see last three columns of Table 5.1 above). One might expect such rates of increase to be roughly related, for instance, to the average growth of a country's foreign trade and other international transactions. The growth of production in general, however, might be equally valuable as a rough guideline, since its long-run maintenance normally involves a parallel [10] expansion in money supply and in the demand liabilities of central banks. These will feel reluctant to see such liabilities increase at a much faster pace than the international reserves

[10] Parallel, but of course not equal: Money supply tends in fact to rise more than proportionately to GNP in the developing countries, until a more advanced stage of development is reached in which substitute forms of liquidity increasingly replace—and reduce the needed growth of—money proper.

needed to underwrite them in a regime of free convertibility and fixed exchange rates.[11]

These broad generalizations require considerable qualifications before they can be applied to any individual country. Faster rates of expansion may be aimed at, in order to reconstitute previously depleted reserve levels, or to finance foreseeable or unpredictable repayments of foreign debts, and so on. Conversely, some countries may prefer, or accept, lower rates of reserve increases if they feel their reserves to be excessively ample already, or if they assign a lower priority to the policy independence and other advantages derivable from high reserve levels than to other national objectives, such as the acceleration of economic development through higher imports, and so on. Expected ability to borrow abroad in case of need, at acceptable financial and political costs, may also play a role in such decisions.

These complex considerations obviously preclude the adoption of any rigid and automatic guidelines as to the desirable rate of increase in world reserves, just as the complexities of national monetary management have always precluded the adoption by any country of any rigid and automatic rules governing desirable increases of national money supply, Milton Friedman notwithstanding. The authorities in charge of either problem cannot escape the responsibility of formulating policies appropriate to varied and unpredictable conditions, in the light of the inflationary or deflationary pressures that it is their task to observe, anticipate, and combat. Yet, one might accept, as a rough and *presumptive* guideline for world reserve increases, over the long run, an *average* growth rate of some 4 percent or 5 percent annually, similar to that suggested by Professor Friedman for national money supply in the United States.

This does not mean, of course, that international monetary policies and institutions could ever underwrite such a growth rate—or any other, for that matter—for any individual country,

---

[11] Professor Machlup arrives at broadly similar conclusions in his illuminating article, "The Need for Monetary Reserves," *Banca Nazionale del Lavoro Quarterly Review* (September, 1966), pp. 3–50.

irrespective of the wisdom or folly of its national policies. What may properly be asked of international monetary management is only to aim at a growth of the world's reserve pool that should enable countries to earn the increases in reserves deemed necessary or desirable to sustain feasible and noninflationary rates of economic activity and development, provided that they follow appropriate policies aiming at the same objective. This would clearly rule out—subject to the qualification below—a negative rate of average growth for world reserves, or even a rate far below the 4 percent or 5 percent presumptive target mentioned above.

Some countries, at least, would then be forced into unnecessarily restrictive or deflationary policies, or into devaluation of their currency, to protect themselves against a raid on their reserves by others, even if all of them geared their policy to reserve increases consonant with economic growth, but higher than available increases in the world reserve pool.

Increases of world reserves even far in excess of 4 percent or 5 percent would not, on the other hand, *force* inflationary policies on any country. They would, however, weaken or eliminate the barriers that reserve losses erect against such policies and that can already be jumped far too easily through trade or exchange restrictions or currency devaluation. Moderation in the expansion of world reserves can at least prevent some countries from financing their own inflationary excesses through unwanted transfers of real resources from the countries that pursue noninflationary —or even simply less inflationary—policies.

A final qualification must be mentioned. High rates of world reserve increases might be necessary, or at least desirable, to make up for an initial shortage or to offset an excessive hoarding of reserves by some countries, due to the pursuit of needlessly deflationary or restrictive policies by them. Lower levels of increase, on the other hand, may prove sufficient if they happen to be supplemented for the countries pursuing reasonable policies by large reserve losses from countries whose reserves were initially excessive, or which pursue inflationary policies at the cost of unwanted reserve losses. The importance of this qualification will be made apparent presently.

Reserve increases, for the world as a whole (see Table 5.1 above), have averaged the very modest level of 2.8 percent a year over the fifteen years 1950–1964 in spite of much higher rates of increase of money supply in most countries and of world trade itself: 6.9 percent for world imports over the same fifteen years, and 8.6 percent over the last five years (1960–1964). Yet the UN indexes of import prices, expressed in dollars—as the reserve increases quoted above—show average price rises of less than 0.5 percent a year for the period as a whole, although substantially higher ones—about 2 percent a year for the developed areas—in the last two years of the period (1963 and 1964).

All in all, world reserve increases well below the presumptive target of 4 percent to 5 percent a year mentioned above do not seem therefore to have elicited any pervasive deflationary tendencies in the world economy. A large part of the explanation, however, lies in the fact that reserve increases for countries other than the United States were sustained at a much higher average level over this period—6.8 percent a year, in fact; that is, practically equal to the growth rate of world trade—by the enormous net reserve losses of the United States. These account indeed for well over two thirds of the gross reserve increases of other countries. This vast redistribution of United States reserves (well in excess of needs at the beginning of the period) to the rest of the world corresponded—partly by design but largely by accident—to the last qualification ventured above regarding the calculation of desirable increases in the pool of world reserves.

It also explains the opposite views put forward by the United States and the United Kingdom, on the one hand, and by the continental European countries, on the other, regarding the adequacy or shortage of international reserves with relation to needs.

THE FACTORS DETERMINING RESERVE CREATION

The factors determining reserve creation under our present monetary system do not bear any relation whatsoever to any rational criteria of legitimate reserve requirements. Gold remains, in theory, the base of the system, but has been increasingly supplemented by foreign-exchange reserves, held primarily in the form of short-term dollar and sterling claims on the United States' and United Kingdom's banks and Treasuries. Net claims of member countries on the IMF—accumulated through gold subscriptions to the Fund's capital and net drawings of a member's currency by other members—constitute a third, and lesser, source of international reserves.[12]

1. Annual increases in gold reserves are determined by the hazards of gold production in the West *minus* the gold absorbed by the arts, industry, hoarding, and speculation, *plus* the gold sales (or *minus* the gold purchases) of the U.S.S.R., China, and other communist countries, in Western markets. The sharp increase of private gold purchases in recent years, and particularly since 1960—more than $1 billion a year, or about 82 percent of gross production—has reduced to a mere trickle the amounts of gold contributed by Western production to the gold reserve pool: about $385 million a year in the 1950's, but only $230 million, on the average, in 1960–1964, representing no more than 10 percent of reserve increases over these years and fluctuating widely between $115 million and $300 million a year. In 1965 and 1966, private purchases actually exceeded new gold production in the noncommunist world. Communist countries' gold sales in Western markets have contributed nearly 50 percent more than Western gold production to central banks' reserves in 1960–1964: about $340 million a year, with lows of $200 million in 1960 and 1962 and as much as $550 million in 1963. These sales dried up entirely in 1966.

2. The contribution of gold to the world reserve pool has been dwarfed by that of foreign-exchange holdings, fed mostly by United States and United Kingdom deficits: more than $7 billion in all over the years 1960–1964, that is, well over $1.5 billion a year, or 65 percent of gross-reserve accumulation over the period as a whole. This dominant source of reserve creation, however, is also the most volatile of all, depending as it does not

[12] IMF credit tranches and standby agreements and bilateral swap and swap standby agreements are classified as "credit facilities" rather than as reserves proper. See below, pp. 105–106.

Table 5.2 Sources of Gross Reserve Increases, 1960–1966

| | IN MILLIONS OF U.S. DOLLARS | | | | | PERCENTAGE CONTRIBUTION TO TOTAL | | |
| | 1960–1966 Range | | Annual Rate | | | | | |
	Min.	Max.	1960–1964	1965	1966	1960–1964	1965	1966
I. World monetary gold	−90	835	575	240	−90	26	18	−7
A. From Soviet sources	—	550	345	400	—	16	30	—
B. Other	−160	300	230	−160	−90	10	−12	−7
II. IMF-BIS transactions	−115	2015	210	2015	50	9	148	4
A. Gold	−905	795	30	795	−905	1	59	−72
B. Reserve positions in the Fund	−365	1220	180	1220	955	8	90	76
III. Foreign exchange	−900	2425	1440	−900	1285	65	−66	103
A. Dollars	−955	1665	1115	45	−955	50	3	−76
B. Sterling	−320	715	165	−320	715	7	−24	57
C. Euro-dollars, Euro-sterling, other, and discrepancies	−630	1525	155	−630	1525	7	−46	122
IV. World gross reserves	320	3405	2225	1355	1250	100	100	100
Foreign exchange reserves of countries other than United States and United Kingdom	−1810	2245	1365	−1810	325	61	−133	26

SOURCES AND NOTES:
See Table 2.2 on p. 46–47.

only on the balance-of-payments fluctuations of the United States and the United Kingdom, but also on the willingness or reluctance of central banks to retain dollars and sterling balances in their reserves rather than to convert them into gold. The contribution of short-term foreign-exchange debts to the world reserve pool was as high, for instance, as $2.4 billion in 1960, owing primarily to huge United States deficits in that year, but actually negative—and for opposite reasons—in 1957 and in 1965. In 1957 ephemeral United States surpluses, associated with the Suez crisis, reduced the *supply* of United States foreign-exchange debts to the world reserve pool by nearly $800 million. In the first half of 1965, on the other hand, a massive contraction of $2000 million in foreign-exchange reserves reflected the massive liquidation of dollar and sterling balances accumulated by central banks over many years past.

3. Net reserve positions in the IMF—*minus* gold purchases or *plus* gold sales by the IMF and the Bank for International Settlements—constitute a third, and lesser, source of reserve increases: about $80 million a year, on the average, in the 1950's, and $210 million a year in 1960–1964, accounting for only 9 percent of total reserve increases over the latter period. This contribution, however, rose dramatically to more than $2000 million, or 148 percent of total reserve increases, in 1965, thus playing a crucial role in quelling the crisis triggered that year by the massive liquidation of foreign-exchange holdings previously accumulated as reserves. It may be called upon to play an increasing role in the future, but can do so only as the result of profound reforms in the present gold-exchange standard, to be discussed in later chapters of this volume.

THE ADJUSTMENT OF SUPPLIES TO NEEDS

It is hardly necessary to conclude that the system described above does not provide any rational method or adjustment of reserve supplies to reserve needs. The hazards of gold production—particularly in a country like the Republic of South Africa, threatened with racial war—of the whims or policies of the Kremlin, of United States and United Kingdom balance-of-payments deficits, of private gold purchases for industrial, artistic, hoarding, and speculative purposes, and of central bankers' preferences as between gold, sterling, and the dollar would hardly be expected to add up to the amounts of reserves needed annually to sustain noninflationary rates of economic expansion.

Total increases in world reserves from these various sources have indeed fluctuated, for instance, from about $320 million in 1962 to about $3400 million in 1963. The basic erraticness and irrationality of such a system of reserve creation are certainly among the most blatant defects calling for correction and reform of the present gold-exchange standard.

The Foreign-Exchange Component of World Reserves

A third and closely related problem is that of the short-run vulnerability and long-run unviability of the large and growing foreign-exchange component of world reserves. It has already been touched upon in the first section of this chapter in connection with the disturbances introduced thereby in the functioning of the adjustment mechanism as far as the reserve-center countries are concerned, and in the second section of the chapter in connection with the erratic impact of foreign-exchange accumulation on the growth of the world reserve pool.

The recurrent sterling and dollar crises of recent years and the parallel spurt in gold speculation bear ample testimony to the seriousness of the problem. The legal and unquestioned right of central banks to convert at any time their dollars, sterling, or other foreign-exchange assets into gold metal was the cornerstone of the gold-exchange standard. Such conversions could be viewed with relative equanimity by the debtor countries as long as the sums involved remained modest in relation to their gold reserves.

This has long ceased to be the case for sterling, however, as catastrophically demonstrated in 1931 and in 1949 and in the periodic sterling crises that have plagued the United Kingdom —and the world—ever since, in spite of the formal or informal agreements aiming at limiting such conversions by members of the sterling area.

It has also ceased to be true for the dollar since the decline in United States gold reserves (from $24.6 billion in 1949 to $13.2 billion in 1966) and the parallel increase in United States liabilities to foreign monetary authorities (from $3 billion to $15 billion over the same period) have impelled the United States to appeal to its creditors to restrain such conversions lest they precipitate not only a dollar crisis, but a crisis of the international monetary system itself. The fundamental nature of the gold-exchange standard shifted thereby from a somewhat haphazard financial habit to a politically oriented system whose effectiveness, however, remains highly precarious in the absence of any agreed-upon norms for concerted policy action and decision-making generally and firmly accepted by all the countries concerned.

This precariousness had long been denounced by economists, but lightly ignored by official experts as long as foreign-exchange reserves continued to grow, at an average pace of about $600 million a year in the 1950's and about $1.5 billion annually over the years 1960–1964. It was, however, dangerously demonstrated by the radical reversal that followed. Instead of accumulating further amounts of foreign exchange, as they had over all previous years, countries other than the two reserve centers liquidated in the short space of six months in the first half of 1965 more than $2.5 billion of their foreign-exchange holdings, switching them into gold ($1.6 billion) and into gold-denominated claims on the IMF ($1 billion) (see line III of Table 5.3). While France was widely denounced as the main culprit in this respect, its gold conversions accounted for less than one half of the total, and its foreign-exchange switches for little more than a third. (See third and first lines of same table.) Very few indeed of the other developed countries refrained from following the French example.

The threat posed to the reserve currencies—and thus to the international reserve system itself—by such sudden and massive conversions would be bound to rise year after year if the growth of world reserves continued to be fed in the future as it has

Table 5.3 Reserve Switches from Foreign Exchange in the First Half of 1965
(in millions of U.S. dollars)

	CHANGES IN RESERVES		RESERVE SWITCHES		
	Foreign Exchange (a)	Total Reserves (b)	From Foreign Exchange [c = a − b = − (d + e)]	To Gold (d)	To IMF Claims (e)
I. Developed countries	−3205	−695	−2510	+1545	+965
A. Industrial Europe	−2130	+15	−2145	+1435	+710
France	−460	+428	−888	+704	+183
Italy	−346	+128	−474	+277	+197
Germany	−706	−430	−276	+130	+146
Belgium	−103	+72	−175	+112	+63
Netherlands	−142	−10	−132	+68	+64
Other countries	−373	−170	−203	+145	+55
B. Other developed countries	−1075	−710	−365	+110	+255
Spain	−260	−61	−199	+164	+34
Canada	−258	−66	−192	+63	+128
Japan	−82	+6	−88	+23	+65
Other countries	−474	−590	+116	−140	+25
II. Less developed countries	+520	+570	−50	+25	+20
III. Nonreserve centers (I + II)	−2685	−125	−2560	+1570	+985
IV. Reserve centers	+500	−435	+935	−1610	+140
A. United States and United Kingdom	+500	−435	+935	−1075	+140
B. IMF-BIS gold				−535	
V. World Total (III + IV)	−2185	−560	−1625	−35	+1120

SOURCE: Calculated from *International Financial Statistics* (October, 1966).

been in the past by the precarious piling up of United States and
United Kingdom IOU's in the books of other central banks. The
Group of Ten unanimously came, more than a year ago, to the
obvious conclusion that this process could not continue indefinitely. Yet its cessation would—as we have seen above—dry
up at the source the foreign-exchange inflows on which the
world has come to depend for as much as two thirds of its total
reserve growth over recent years.

The gold-exchange standard mechanism thus carries within
itself the seeds of its own destruction. Its process of reserve creation is not only highly erratic and increasingly vulnerable, but
is bound to lead, sooner or later, either to a sudden collapse à
la 1931 or to a gradual tapering off of the reserve increases necessary to sustain feasible rates of growth in world trade and
production.

6

The Course of
Negotiations on International
Monetary Reform

The reforms needed for the survival of an orderly international monetary system have been, over the last five years, a constant topic for studies and negotiations at the highest level among national and international experts and officials. A number of steps have been taken already, and served the crucial function of gaining time for the more protracted discussions necessary to agree on the fundamental reforms whose long-run indispensability is no longer denied. Bilateral swap and swap standby agreements have been concluded by the United States with a dozen major countries, in order to provide, with maximum speed and discretion, short-term credits in case of need. Agreements have also been reached among the main central banks to coordinate somewhat their interventions in the London gold market. Medium-term bonds, carrying guarantees against exchange risks, have been placed by the United States with a number of central banks in order to bolster their willingness to refrain from excessive conversions of unrequired dollars into gold. Recurrent sterling crises have been plugged by large purchases of sterling by central banks, undertaken on a multilateral but extremely short-term basis and liquidated a few months later through British drawings on the IMF (sterling claims being exchanged, in effect, for claims on the Fund). The General Arrangements to Borrow were negotiated to replenish the Fund's holdings in the currencies of the major creditor countries, when depleted as a result of these and other operations. Finally, Fund quotas were substantially increased in 1966.

These and other measures and policy actions have enabled the world to live dangerously over the last few years, but they are obviously far short of the reforms needed to consolidate and improve the long-run functioning of the international monetary system and which are now under active consideration by the IMF, the Group of Ten, and UNCTAD.

An Emerging Consensus

The first report of the Group of Ten, in August, 1964, and the *1964 Annual Report* of the IMF gave most encouraging signs of the revolutionary progress of official thinking on the major issues involved. The diagnosis of the problem revealed a unanimous consensus regarding the basic defects of the present system, very much along the lines summarized in the preceding chapter. Both reports agreed that gold production had long been, and would remain, vastly insufficient to assure a satisfactory growth of world reserves and that the United States dollar could not be expected to continue to fill the whole gap between available gold supplies and the minimum reserve requirements of an expanding world economy.[1]

Both reports were still somewhat vague and tentative with regard to the exact nature of the reforms that might be proposed

---

[1] Subparagraphs 25 (a) and (b) of the *Annex Prepared by Deputies* and p. 31 of the *1964 IMF Report*. Sterling was not mentioned in this connection in either report.

later. Yet agreement was also reached on a number of important conclusions, both negative and positive.

Among the possible solutions of the problem, two were firmly and unanimously discarded at the very outset of the investigation: a revaluation of the price of gold and a recourse to flexible exchange rates. The communiqué of October 2, 1963, recording the establishment of the Group of Ten had stated: "In reviewing the longer-run prospects, the Ministers and Governors agreed that the underlying structure of the present monetary system—based on fixed exchange rates and the established price of gold—has proven its value as the foundation for present and future arrangements." The same view was quoted and reaffirmed in the August, 1964 report.

Deputies also rejected as a solution any proliferation of the reserve currencies: "There is no immediate prospect of any other currency assuming the function of an international reserve currency. Indeed, at the present juncture such a development could raise problems without substantially strengthening the system." [2] By opening the door to reserve shifts from one currency into another—as well as from currencies into gold—such a proliferation would *increase* the instability of the system.

"Recently developed bilateral facilities for swaps and *ad hoc* support operations have already, in periods of stress, been effective in maintaining orderly conditions for international payments in the exchange market. They should . . . continue to play an essential role . . ." Extremely important, however, are the two passages deleted by me from this quotation and now cited separately to highlight their importance: *"within a suitable framework for multilateral surveillance"* and *"for short-term purposes."* [3] The IMF report spelled out more bluntly the meaning of "short-term" by stating that bilateral swap arrangements "are not appropriate to meet disequilibria for more than a few

[2] Subparagraph 25 (c) of the *Annex Prepared by Deputies*. Since this follows a subparagraph (b) referring to the reserve role of the dollar alone, the words "any other currency" mean "any currency other than the dollar" and would imply a recognition by all—including Britain—that sterling has already ceased to be acceptable as a truly international reserve currency.

[3] Subparagraph 25 (f) of the *Annex Prepared by Deputies*.

months." The Fund also stressed the fact that "the possibility of undertaking such arrangements is in practice open only to a relatively restricted group of countries. By contrast, multilateral institutions can extend the scope of their operations to a world-wide membership." [4]

Both reports, therefore, clearly rejected bilateral arrangements of this sort as meeting the need for long-run, permanent reserve increases. They were grouped, in the deputies' report, with the IMF transactions themselves, not as sources of reserve creation, but as "credit facilities" that "will continue to play an essential part in financing imbalances. Particularly for *medium-term* credit, the IMF fulfills a valuable and unique function and should continue in its central role." [5]

Turning now to the more positive and constructive recommendations of the two reports, we must take notice of two bold recommendations unanimously endorsed by both.

The first is that

> *the need may in time be felt for some additional kind of reserve asset. We think it would be timely to investigate the problems raised by the creation and use of such an asset, the possible forms it might take and the institutional aspects associated with it.*[6]

While this revolutionary conclusion was understandably couched in extremely cautious language, a "Study Group on the Creation of Reserve Assets" had nevertheless already been established by the time the report was issued.

The second major conclusion of the Group of Ten was that

> *the process of adjustment and the need for international liquidity are closely interrelated . . . The need being to supply sufficient*

---

[4] IMF Report, p. 33.

[5] Subparagraph 25 (e) of the *Annex Prepared by Deputies.* Italics are mine. It was also noted later, however, under subparagraph 25 (g) that "when credits provided by monetary authorities are availed of by the debtor, a form of reserve asset is created in the process." This qualification opens the door to the use of the IMF for reserve-creation purposes, but would, of course, require new resources and procedures to meet this objective—unforeseen in the Articles of Agreement—and particularly to avoid—or compensate for—the "reserve destruction" implicit in medium-term repayment obligations.

[6] Subparagraph 25 (d) of the *Annex Prepared by Deputies.*

> *liquidity to finance temporary payments imbalances without*
> *frustrating the required process of international adjustment in in-*
> *dividual countries, it is desirable to bring under multilateral review*
> *and appraisal the various means of financing surpluses or deficits.*

Various steps were therefore taken by the group to "provide a basis for multilateral surveillance of the various elements of liquidity creation." [7]

The Managing Director of the IMF, Pierre-Paul Schweitzer, rightly interpreted this conclusion, in several speeches, as indicating "the emerging consensus among the international community that the creation of international liquidity, like the creation of domestic liquidity, should become a matter of deliberate decision."

Negotiating Divergences among the Ten

The agreement skillfully reached and worded in the August, 1964, report of the Group of Ten disguised, however, fundamental differences between the two reserve currency debtors—the United States and the United Kingdom—and the major reserve-currency creditors—the continental European countries, particularly France.

BASIC DIFFERENCES

The reserve-currency debtors focused attention on the shortage of liquidity and viewed any new reserve asset to be created only as a *supplement,* but not as a *substitute,* for already existing forms of liquidity creation. It would be absurd, they argued, to put upon this new and untried liquidity asset any more burden than would prove strictly necessary. As long as, and insofar as, dollars and pounds could fill the gap between insufficient gold supplies and legitimate liquidity requirements, this traditional and familiar form of reserve holding should be encouraged rather

[7] Paragraphs 5, 25 (h), and 37 of the *Annex Prepared by Deputies.*

than discouraged. The new reserve asset should be used only to supplement it in case of need.

The Europeans, on the other hand—particularly the French Minister of Finance Valéry Giscard d'Estaing—disagreed both with this diagnosis and with the prescription following from it. The major defect of the present system of reserve creation is its *haphazardness,* which may trigger inflationary excesses as well as deflationary shortages, and has indeed done so in recent years and continues to do so today, owing primarily to its monetization of huge and persistent deficits of the reserve-currency countries. The mere insertion of an additional type of reserve asset into the system would not remedy this situation and might indeed aggravate it if it were used, under powerful political pressure by the United States and/or the United Kingdom, to mop up *ex post* the dollar and sterling balances arising from further United States and United Kingdom deficits whenever central banks refused to accumulate and retain them voluntarily as reserves.

These economic arguments of the French Finance Minister were blown up into a major political argument by President de Gaulle in his press conference of February 4, 1965. Why should the two richest countries of the world be allowed to monopolize the benefits of international-reserve creation for the financing of their own deficits? Why should the Bank of France be expected to participate—by its purchases of dollars—in the financing of United States policies in which France has no voice and with which she might be in fundamental disagreement? Are not the United States deficits ascribable, at least in part, to the flurry of United States private investments abroad (substituting United States for French ownership), to United States assistance to Chiang Kai-shek, to the escalation of the war in Southeast Asia, and so on?

If new reserve assets are to be created, it should be by joint decisions, for agreed-upon purposes, and to *replace*—rather than merely *supplement*—the economically irrational and politically unacceptable privilege now enjoyed in this respect by the two Anglo-Saxon currencies.

A second major source of disagreement within the Group of

Ten related to the distribution of voting power in the collective decision-making process to be adopted. Britain and the United States, finding themselves in a small minority in the Group of Ten, argued that since the decisions called for would affect the interests of the world at large, they should be taken by a world body, the IMF, rather than by any restricted group increasingly dubbed "the rich nations' club." The countries of the European Economic Community, on the other hand, were unwilling to run the risk of being too easily outvoted in the Fund's executive board in which they held only about one fifth of the voting power while contributing currently more than 70 percent of the resources actually used by the Fund. They were understandably reluctant to abandon vital decisions as to the size and management of their additional contributions to an executive board in which present—and prospective?—net borrowers control nearly two thirds of the total voting power (see Table 6.1).

Table 6.1 Net Fund Positions and Voting Power
(in percentage of total net claims and voting power)

	Net Claims, or Debts (−)[1]	Voting Rights[2]	
		By Country	By Executive Director
I. Net claims on IMF	100	33.5	36.1
A. European Community	72	16.0	20.8
B. Other developed areas	28	17.5	15.3
II. Net Debts to IMF	64	66.5	63.9
A. United States and United Kingdom	49	33.2	33.2
B. Less-developed areas	16	33.3	30.7
III. IMF gold	43	x	x
IV. IMF profits = II + III − I	7	x	x

NOTES:

1. As of September 30, 1965.

2. As of April 30, 1965. Since the voting power of small countries is pooled and exercised in fact by an Executive Director elected jointly by them, but who casts a single vote for all the countries that elected him, the latter column redistributes voting rights in accordance with the nationality of the Executive Directors.

The Europeans thus favored retaining control within the Group of Ten itself, in which they commanded a clear majority. The most conservative of the countries' representatives even insisted, in spite of this majority, that future decisions would continue to require a unanimous vote, thus allowing even a single country to veto any creation of new reserve assets that it might regard as inflationary.

COMPROMISES AND DISSENTS[8]

These basic, and other, differences are reflected in the wide diversity of proposals discussed by the Group of Ten and of the objections that have so far blocked the adoption of any of them.

The arguments pro and con various solutions were painstakingly catalogued in the *Report of the Study Group on the Creation of Reserve Assets* (May 31, 1965), better known as the *Ossola Report,* from the name of its able and diplomatic chairman, Rinaldo Ossola of the Bank of Italy. The preparation and discussion of this report were the main accomplishments of the Group of Ten in its second year of operation.

A third year was devoted to the far more difficult task of discovering some basis of agreement for common recommendations acceptable to all the members of the Group. The report of the Deputies attempting this tour de force was presented to the ministers on July 8, 1966, by their chairman, Dr. Otmar Emminger, of the Bundesbank, and will be referred to below as the *Emminger Report*.

The process of negotiation from which these two reports emerged inevitably centered on reaching a *politically acceptable compromise* between conflicting national viewpoints rather than the most *logical solution* to the economic problem of international reserve management viewed in the abstract.

The so-called CRU proposal, initially advanced by the French, was seized upon as the most promising path toward such a compromise. *Composite reserve units* would be created, when

[8] I strongly urge all but the most obdurate of my readers to skip this gloomy, bewildering, and confusing account of ephemeral "negotiating positions" and to resume their reading on p. 119 below.

needed, in amounts to be agreed upon among the Ten themselves, and distributed among them in strict proportion to each
country's gold reserves, against equivalent contributions of their
respective national currencies to a common currency pool desig-
nated to "back" the new units created. Later reserve settlements
among the participating countries would be effected through
simultaneous transfers of gold and CRU reserves, in accordance
with the overall proportions of these two types of reserve assets
outstanding at the time of such settlements as a result of the
cumulative creation of CRU's in the past. Dollar, sterling, and
other foreign-exchange balances would be excluded from such
settlements among the participating countries, and outstanding
balances would be gradually replaced also by CRU balances.
Other countries, regarded as belonging to the dollar or sterling
areas, could continue, however, to accumulate and retain dollar
or sterling balances in reserves if they so wished. Finally, all decisions relating to the creation of new composite reserve units
would be taken by unanimous vote, and each country would retain the right to convert at any time into gold its accumulated
CRU balances, even though this would presumably entail, in effect, its withdrawal from the system and, if imitated by other
members, might trigger its enforced liquidation.[9]

The French plan seems to have been substantially endorsed
by the Dutch, but acceptable only in part to the other countries
of the European Economic Community. All of them agreed on
the need to erect strong barriers against inflationary abuses of
any new technique for reserve creation and to isolate the creation of "earned," "owned," "unconditional" reserves "to hold,"
from the creation of "borrowed," "conditional" reserves, "to
spend" for the financing of any individual country's balance-of-
payments deficits. They also wished to keep the creation of new

[9] While the CRU technique as such was closely modeled upon the original proposals of E. M. Bernstein, they were inserted by the latter in an extremely expansionist—rather than conservative—framework, preserving a large role for
dollar and/or sterling balances and supplemented by substantial increases in the
amount and automaticity of IMF lending. See my article "The Bizarre Proposals of Dr. Bernstein for International Monetary Reform," *Kyklos* Vol. XVII
(1964), No. 3, pp. 328–345 (reproduced in my *The World Money Maze* [New
Haven, Conn.: Yale University Press, 1966], pp. 327–340).

reserve assets under the effective control of the Ten, but recognized on the other hand the desirability of inserting it within the worldwide framework of the IMF. German and Italian representatives, moreover, showed particular interest for proposals aiming at a more "harmonious" composition of reserves as between gold and foreign exchange. While logically attractive, of course, this position also corresponded to their own interest, since they held a relatively smaller proportion of their total reserves in gold than the other EEC countries, and a larger one in "unrequited" foreign exchange balances. Finally, Belgium pressed particularly for the adoption of legal techniques strengthening—and making more obvious—the fully liquid and transferable character of the new reserve assets and their unquestionable eligibility as a normal component of monetary reserves.

The United States, the United Kingdom, Sweden, Canada, and Japan generally stressed the need for reserve expansion and for weighted IMF voting rather than for unanimous decisions restricted to the Group of Ten. The first two countries—particularly the United States—insisted especially on the need to avoid any weakening of the traditional role of their own currencies in the process of reserve creation. The British, however, were more willing than the United States to grant exchange-value, and even full gold-weight, guarantees on reserve-currency holdings, to the extent necessary to induce foreign central banks to accumulate and retain them in settlement of their future surpluses and to refrain from "destabilizing" and "deflationary" conversions of such holdings into gold metal.

Strong objections were also raised by several countries against the rigid link that the French plan wished to establish between gold and the new reserve asset, with regard both to the initial distribution of newly created assets among members and to their later use in balance-of-payments settlements. Such a link was regarded as essential by the French to give confidence in the new asset and preserve, rather than frustrate, the "disciplinary" pressures of settlements crucial to the classical mechanism of balance-of-payments adjustment. The opponents of this French thesis feared that such a link would trigger a rush into gold by countries previously willing to hold a large portion of their reserves in other forms, particularly in dollars or sterling. They even viewed with some justification indeed this feature of the French proposal as tantamount to a "disguised increase in the gold price for the countries concerned." [10]

These opposite views hardened into a monetary "cold war," culminating in the "summit clash" between President de Gaulle and President Johnson in their respective press conferences of February, 1965, and in massive gold conversions by the French and other European countries ($2.3 billion in nine months, from October, 1964, through June, 1965).

Some signs of a renewed effort toward negotiations and compromises emerged, during the following months, from the European tour of Secretary Fowler in the summer, the IMF annual meeting in September, and the reunion of the Group of Ten in Paris in November.

A communiqué of the ministers and governors of the Group of Ten, issued on September 28, 1965, revealed three substantial concessions of the Europeans to the Anglo-American points of view:

1. Agreement that the General Arrangements to Borrow should be renewed for a second period of four years (from October, 1966, to October, 1970), subject to review and adaptation in October, 1968, or later.

2. Agreement to intensify, in a first phase, their discussions of "contingency planning" regarding the

improvements needed in the international monetary system, including arrangements for the future creation of reserve assets, as

[10] *Ossola Report*, p. 56. If, for example, new reserve assets were created in amounts equal to 20 percent of the participating countries' gold reserves and used in the same proportion to supplement gold transfers in subsequent balance-of-payments settlements, the net effect would be the same as if $100 in gold were now worth to them $120. Moreover, the right of members to withdraw from the system at will and to convert their accumulated CRU balances into gold (see p. 111 above) might, if exercised on a sufficient scale, force in effect an open change in the official gold price at a later stage. In that case the consequent revaluation profits would be exactly equal to the national currencies earmarked as backing for the system and would permit canceling corresponding bookkeeping entries.

and when needed, so as to permit adequate provision for the reserve needs of the world economy. The Deputies should report to the Ministers in the spring of 1966 on the progress of their deliberations and the scope of agreement that they have found.

3. Recognition that

as soon as a basis for agreement on essential points has been reached, it will be necessary to proceed from this first phase to a broader consideration of the questions that affect the world economy as a whole. They [the ministers and governors] have agreed that it would be very useful to seek ways and means by which the efforts of the Executive Board of the Fund and those of the Deputies of the Group of Ten can be directed toward a consensus as to desirable lines of action, and they have instructed their Deputies to work out during the coming year, in close consultation with the Managing Director of the Fund, procedures to achieve this aim, with a view to preparing for the final enactment of any new arrangements at an appropriate forum for international discussions.

The statement of the French Minister of Finance at the IMF meeting was largely directed at drawing support from the under-developed countries and relaxed, for the first time, the rigid link that France had previously advocated between the new reserve assets and gold:

An agreement could be made to establish a relationship between the creating of additional reserve assets and the organizing of the markets for certain commodities. . . . It is conceivable that a distribution of additional reserve assets could take into account, among various criteria, the actual efforts made by each country in favor of developing countries.

Convergent—and obviously concerted—statements of the spokesmen for the other EEC countries put considerable emphasis on another aspect of the problem, which had been carefully avoided throughout most of the previous debates. Governor Holtrop, of the Netherlands, referred to "the instability of the system, which is partly due to the freedom of conversion from one reserve medium into another." He had himself applauded this instability at the IMF Vienna Meeting of 1961 as a protection both against excessive and inflationary accumulation of foreign-currency reserves and against their massive and deflationary liquidation into gold metal.

> *Now, with the benefit of recent experience, there is reason again to ask the question whether it might not be preferable to replace —at least within a limited group of industrialized countries— liberty of action in regard to switching from one reserve medium to another by certain rules of behavior with respect to the proportion of different reserve media to be held in official reserves. And also to investigate whether the present unilateral responsibility of reserve currency countries for the consequences of fluctuations in the total volume of reserve currency held by third countries in official and nonofficial balances, might not be replaced by some collective sharing of that responsibility. I am convinced that the solution of these two problems should form an integral part of any future reform of the international monetary system.*

Governor Blessing, of Germany, chimed in with the view that "the most acute problem is not the artificial creation of new liquidity, but rather the danger that existing liquidity could be destroyed by a sudden run on one country or a group of countries."

The most detailed, concrete, and constructive discussion of this problem was that of Minister Colombo of Italy. Stressing also the urgent need to protect the stability of the international monetary system against the immediate danger that the volume of reserves may contract as a result of sudden or massive switches from reserve currencies into gold, he advocated concerted moves toward a more harmonious composition of reserves as between gold and credit assets, and the conversion of unrequired currency balances either into IMF claims or mutual currency accounts.

Finally, Governor Ansiaux, of Belgium, propounded changes in the IMF Articles of Agreement designed to enhance the acceptability and attractiveness of credit claims on the IMF as international reserves for central banks: exchange-value guarantees, unconditional and liquid usability for balance-of-payments settlements, free transferability, and so on.

The statements of the United States and United Kingdom governors were far less explicit. Secretary Fowler emphasized that "the United States is wedded to no specific plan, . . . [We] are impressed with the wide variety of technical possibilities which have been developed in the writings of distinguished economists here and abroad . . ." Chancellor Callaghan

> [made] it clear that we in the United Kingdom are ready to consider with an open mind all of these proposals that have been brought forward. The major requirement in my view is that we should make a maximum effort to secure the agreement of all parties legitimately concerned on the way the international monetary system should develop. There is no advantage to the world in all of us holding fast to our particular preferences for achieving such evolution if the result should be that we were not ready to meet the need deliberately to create more reserves as that need arises.

These indications of flexibility in the United States and the United Kingdom approaches to future negotiations were reinforced by the publication of former Under Secretary of the Treasury Roosa's volume *Monetary Reform for the World Economy* (New York: Harper and Row, 1965), which, rightly or wrongly, was widely regarded as reflecting the trend of official thinking in the United States and suggested a possible relaxation of former United States opposition to exchange-value or even gold-value guarantees on United States indebtedness to central banks; and to special voting-power provisions reinforcing the influence of prospective European contributors in all decisions regarding the size and management of any additional reserve asset to be created in the future.

An American plan was indeed finally submitted to the Group of Ten in the winter of 1965–1966. It is summarized as Scheme B in Annex I (pp. 20–24) of the *Emminger Report,* together with a British proposal (Scheme C), two alternative IMF proposals

(Schemes D and E) and Emminger's own compromise proposal (Scheme A).

A common characteristic of all these "schemes" is the highly technical details in which they express, or bury, the fundamental divergences of views and objectives reviewed above. For instance, conflicting choices—and attempted compromises and marriages —between "reserve units" and "special reserve drawing rights" disguise different preferences as to the conditional or unconditional character of the new reserve asset for the debtor countries, the distribution and automaticity of the creditors' lending commitments, the severity or laxity of repayment obligations, the pattern of voting rights, the exposure of reserve currencies to liquidation and gold redemption, and so on.

Any meaningful account and explanation of ephemeral and incompatible negotiating positions and compromises on these technical issues would overtax the patience of most readers, and would almost certainly have become largely obsolete before its appearance in print. I shall confine myself, therefore, to a few brief comments about the more recent and significant developments in the underlying power struggle that will, in the end, determine the outcome of the negotiations.

In a first phase—until April, 1967—the clash between the French and the American negotiators stimulated a mutual escalation and hardening of positions on both sides. The French formally withdrew their own CRU plan from the negotiating table and brought into the open the question of a gold revaluation as a long-run solution to any future liquidity shortage. This was understandably interpreted by the United States as a direct attack against the dollar and a sequel to previous large-scale conversions of dollars into gold by the French, spurring on similar action by other countries. The United States reacted by giving up any hope it might ever have entertained to assuage French opposition to its own proposals, and stepped up its efforts to accelerate a "consensus" among other countries. It also exerted its immense economic and political bargaining power upon these countries to deter them from converting into gold the dollars accruing to them from current United States deficits,

and particularly from the splurge of American direct investments in Europe, the deployment of American troops abroad,
and the war in Vietnam.

These pressures, and the threat of "unilateral action" by
the United States susceptible of "undermining the international
monetary system" itself (Secretary Fowler's speech in Pebble
Beach, California, March 16, 1967), were widely interpreted,
here and abroad, as possible forerunners of dollar inconvertibility—whether *de jure,* or *de facto* by gentlemen's agreements—
confronting other countries with an awesome choice indeed. Any
countries that yielded to the United States would become passive
members of an inconvertible dollar area and finance—through
dollar accumulation—whatever deficits might result from policies
unilaterally decided in Washington or from the failure of such
policies. On the other hand, any country that refused to purchase
the overflow of inconvertible dollars from the market would see
its own currency go up in value and subject its own firms and
producers to increasing competition, at home and abroad, by the
firms and producers of the "dollar area" countries.

This dilemma was particularly alarming to the European
Economic Community countries, since each might be inclined—
or persuaded—to adopt one term of this alternative rather than
the other, at the risk of disrupting the exchange-rate stability of
their currencies vis-à-vis one another, and of endangering, as a
consequence, their hard-won agreements on trade liberalization
and, particularly, on uniform agricultural prices and policies.
The threat of such crises thus spurred the EEC countries to reach
agreement on a common negotiating position acceptable to the
United States as an alternative to "going it alone."

This involved considerable concessions by the French to the
views of their partners in the Community. They now recognized
implicitly that some "mergers" of sovereignty through *joint* IMF
decisions were the only realistic—and a far preferable—alternative to *either* international monetary chaos and warfare *or* much
vaster surrenders of sovereignty to the United States. They expressed their willingness to increase substantially their lending
commitments to the IMF and to accept larger delegations of

authority to its Management and Executive Board, subject only to moderate and reasonable claims to a fairer apportionment of voting rights. While expressing a strong preference for new "conditional" rather than "unconditional" drawing rights, they even withdrew their objections to the latter in order to reach final agreement on joint EEC proposals.

Paradoxically, the French and their EEC partners thus ended by endorsing the initial preference of the United States for an IMF solution, while the United States continued to favor the "reserve unit" technique initially proposed by the French and belatedly accepted—with considerable modifications, however—by the United States and other participating countries. At first view, this double turnabout in previous negotiating positions has merely substituted a new kind of impasse for the previous one. A more optimistic and constructive appraisal fortunately seems to prevail, for the moment at least, among the negotiators. The former intransigent attitudes and highhanded tactics of both France and the United States fed on one another and had reduced practically to nought the chances for a *general* agreement. These chances have now been rekindled, and are spurring new efforts to reach a compromise acceptable to all. Whether these cautious hopes are justified or not will be far clearer to the reader when this book reaches him, than it is now to the author at the time he delivers this manuscript to the publisher.

The IMF Proposals

The views of the IMF itself on a problem so central to its responsibilities and objectives are set forth most authoritatively, but also most cautiously and guardedly, in the 1964, 1965, and 1966 Annual Reports of its Executive Board. The Executive Directors, however, could hardly be expected to disagree with the positions adopted in the Group of Ten negotiations by the countries of which they are themselves the representatives in the IMF. Nor could they be expected to agree on any specific proposals on which their countries were still at loggerheads in these negotiations. Given these constraints, the 1964 and 1965 comments of the Executive Directors may be regarded as remarkably positive and suggestive.

They refer to the focus placed by the Group of Ten studies "on the deliberate creation of reserves by collective international action in the light of an appraisal of the general need for reserves rather than on their creation in response to immediate needs of particular countries for balance of payments assistance." [11] While recognizing that "the task of influencing the total level of world reserves could be carried out by a new institution . . . ," they stress the arguments that can reasonably be offered to support the view that "a matter which is of concern to all countries should be handled in an institution that has been organized as an instrument of financial cooperation on a worldwide basis." [12]

After noting the agreements already reached, or in prospect, regarding quota increases and the renewal of the General Arrangements to Borrow, they focus on the specific contributions that the Fund could make toward the supply of "unconditional" liquidity.[13] Unconditional liquidity is already created, under the present system of operations of the Fund, for any member whose "automatic" gold tranche, or reserve position, with the Fund increases as a result of drawings of its currency by other members. This creation of unconditional liquidity, however, occurs "only as a by-product of drawings, and in amounts that are small compared with total quotas." [14]

Three new techniques are mentioned as possible ways for the Fund to systematically expand unconditional liquidity if and when this is deemed desirable.

The first would be to enlarge automatic borrowing rights beyond the gold tranche, into some portion of the present credit tranches. The second would be "to substitute for a portion of

---

[11] *1965 Annual Report*, pp. 15–18.

[12] *Ibid.*

[13] The distinction properly drawn by the Group of Ten between the creation of liquidity and the provision of credit facilities was referred to on p. 106 above.

[14] *1964 Annual Report*, p. 38.

the gold subscription to the Fund an alternative method of payment, e.g., by means of gold certificates." [15]

Either of these two methods, however, would enlarge automatic drawing rights on the Fund without supplying it with the resources necessary to honor such drawings in the creditor currencies needed by members for balance-of-payments settlements. By the end of October, 1965, for instance, the Fund had already been forced to replenish its depleted holdings of EEC currencies through gold sales and GAB borrowings for a total amount of more than $1600 million. Yet in spite of this, its total holdings of these currencies had dropped to less than $500 million. Any enlargement of the Fund's lending commitments might quickly prove unsustainable and illusory, therefore, if it were not accompanied by a parallel expansion of its access to the creditor currencies needed to finance such lendings.

The third technique suggested by the Fund is directly inspired by the nature of the problem to be solved, that is, the prospective shortage of liquidity, rather than by efforts to meet it indirectly as a by-product of its traditional lending operations. Fund investments, in currency or in gold, would be undertaken on the initiative of the Fund, rather than of any individual country, for the very purpose of creating liquidity rather than in response to any particular balance-of-payments need. They might be distributed among all member countries or on a selective basis to support jointly agreed-upon policies.

The resources needed to finance such investments would be provided under negotiated lines of credit, by "deposits" according to suitable criteria, or in other ways.

> *In order that the Fund's investment should in fact increase unconditional liquidity, it would be essential that members treat the resulting liquid claims on the Fund as reserves. . . . The precise nature of these Fund liabilities (i.e. members' reserve assets) would have to be worked out, but could include at least the following: (1) the facility of the asset to be cashed in for useful currency at least as freely as gold tranche positions or, alternatively, to be transferred directly to other members; (2) a gold-value*

[15] *Ibid.*

guarantee; (3) interest at a modest rate reflecting the gold value of the claim. It will be noted that claims under the General Arrangements to Borrow have these three characteristics.[16]

The Fund's views, however, could not but be influenced by the trend in the Group of Ten discussions (see the section "Negotiating Divergences among the Ten," pp. 107–119 above) toward a CRU type of solution distributing automatically among members, on the basis of so-called objective criteria, whatever amounts of fiduciary reserves *they*—rather than the IMF as such—decided to create. This shift toward automatism and special voting provisions is reflected in two proposals advanced by the Managing Director (Pierre-Paul Schweitzer), and summarized on pp. 19–20 of the *1966 Annual Report* of the IMF and in Annex I of the *Emminger Report* (Scheme D and Scheme E).[17]

The first scheme would create *special reserve drawing rights* unconditionally available to meet payments deficits. These would be financed by the parallel extension of credit lines to the Fund by members, each in its own currency, but in amounts *at least equal* to the drawing rights assigned to it. The credit lines granted by prospective creditors would have to be sufficiently large, in fact, to back the potential drawings of prospective borrowers. This would make it necessary to require that "a special majority of certain specified members" be included in the weighted voting in favor of creating any new reserve drawing rights. The credit lines theoretically extended *to* the Fund by prospective deficit countries would indeed remain largely dormant and theoretical. If large deficits by a large number of countries continued to concentrate—as in all the postwar years of successive dollar shortage and dollar glut—on a very few surplus countries, the contributions of the latter would have to be very large indeed to finance the borrowings of others without reverting to inconvertibility, or even bilateralism, in world trade and payments.

[16] *1964 Annual Report,* p. 39 and *1965 Annual Report,* p. 19.

[17] The 1966 report notes that "The Executive Directors have held preliminary discussions on these proposals, . . . but have thus far not attempted to reach any conclusions. . . . The Executive Directors intend to continue discussions on these proposals."

The main virtue ascribed to this first scheme (see p. 14 of the *1966 Annual Report* of the Fund) is that it "could be implemented without amendment of the Articles of Agreement and employs techniques which are already well tried in the Fund's own experience." This argument may be not as strong as it sounds if one reflects that all participants in the scheme would have to vote for it in any case—whether this be considered an "amendment of the Articles of Agreement" or not—and that the scheme obviously introduces new techniques that have neither been "well tried," nor even contemplated, in those sacrosanct Articles of Agreement.

In any case, a second scheme is presented as alternative to the first, or to be used concurrently with it, or to substitute for it in time. This second scheme would achieve the same results as the first, but through "reserve units," rather than through "special reserve drawing rights." Reserve units would be transferable directly between members, without intervention by the Fund. To insure the fully multilateral usability of the new unit, each member would agree to accept it in payment and hold it up to three times its cumulative allocation. Units transferred to a member in excess of this "holding limit" could be shifted to other members in accordance with supplementary "rules intended to distribute *equitably* (italics mine) among net creditor countries those units disposed of by other countries in order to meet payments deficits" (paragraph 26 of Annex I to the *Emminger Report*). This "equitable" distribution would presumably entail, in the opinions of Mr. Schweitzer and the Fund's Staff, the use of criteria aiming at "bringing about a general proportionality between holdings of the new reserves and other forms of reserves" (see *1966 Annual Report*, p. 20). In plainer language, this would mean that surplus countries should accumulate a uniform proportion of their total reserves in the form of the new reserve medium to be created.[18]

[18] I explained, when presenting this suggestion for the first time in *Gold and the Dollar Crisis* (New Haven, Conn.: Yale University Press, 1960), p. 106, how it would solve most simply and directly the problems for which far more complex and incomplete answers are still debated today by the Group of Ten and the IMF. With adequate provisions regarding the overall amount of new reserve

Other suggestions of Mr. Schweitzer would apply equally to both of his proposals. All members of the IMF should have the opportunity to participate in the *distribution* of new reserves—pro rata of their Fund quota or some other measure of the relative economic size of each country—but special voting powers should be assigned to the "stronger" currency countries able, and called upon, to finance the system. The recipient countries would also be required to use their new reserve allocations to repay their outstanding credit-tranche borrowings from the Fund.

One senses in some passages of the *Report* devoted to this question (particularly pp. 16–17) a note of regret at the objections raised by the Group of Ten against the alternative and more flexible solutions previously advanced by the Fund. The *1966 Report* of the Fund clearly aims at a negotiating consensus, along the lines insisted upon by its major Group of Ten members, rather than at continued insistence on the solutions that the Fund's Staff and Management would regard as most rational and desirable ways to meet the future problem of international monetary management.

The Report of the UNCTAD's Experts

The Report of the group of experts[19] appointed by the UNCTAD draws essentially—as pointed out in paragraph 70—on the studies under way in the Fund and in the Group of Ten, facilitating thereby the dialogue between them and the underdeveloped

---

assets to be created, and the guarantees to be attached to them, such holdings would be as safe and liquid—or more—as any other reserve media, and their distribution among countries would adjust automatically to fluctuations in overall reserves and balance of payments. This would obviate the need for arbitrary guesswork, designed to achieve similar objectives, in the proposals reviewed above: that is, the need for larger (by how much)? credit lines to the IMF by stronger (which?) members, or of the acceptance by them of a specified holding limit of reserve units equal to a multiple (which?) of their cumulative allocation.

Further suggestions to increase the negotiability of this proposed commitment are presented on pp. 114–115 of *Gold and the Dollar Crisis,* and on pp. 146–164 below.

[19] *International Monetary Issues and the Developing Countries,* Doc. TD/B/32 and TD/B/C.3/6, November 1, 1965.

countries, which had, up to then, played little or no role in a negotiation in which their interests are also vitally involved.

It gives only lukewarm endorsement, "as a preliminary or interim stage in the process of deliberate reserve creation," to the Fund's suggestion for "the extension of automatic drawing rights, of the type now applied in the gold tranche, into the credit tranches" (paragraphs 84 and 85) and reserves its main fire for the ways and means ensuring maximum benefits for the under-developed countries from the setting up of a mechanism "devised for the 'deliberate creation of reserves by collective international action in the light of an appraisal of the general need for reserves,' in place of primary reliance [as of now] upon largely fortuitous accretions of monetary stocks of gold and upon reserve currency holdings arising from the deficits of reserve centers" (paragraph 67, a).

While the words quoted in this passage are taken from the *1965 Annual Report* of the Fund (p. 15), the concrete mechanism later propounded by the UNCTAD experts is essentially based on the French CRU proposal, considerably revamped to fit the underdeveloped countries' objectives. Participation would be extended beyond the Group of Ten to all members of the Fund (paragraph 77) and even to "countries not now members, if they are prepared to take part in both the benefits and the obligations of new monetary arrangements designed to serve the interests of the international community as a whole" (paragraph 68, d).

The mechanism is operated by the Fund, rather than by a separate agent, and "*presumably* [italics mine] the rule of unanimity gives way to weighted voting." The CRU units are re-baptized 'Fund Units' in the new context. "Otherwise the system could conceivably be reproduced exactly as before" (paragraph 74).

That is to say, Fund Units, endowed with a gold guarantee, would be created in amounts determined each year by the participating countries, and distributed among them in accordance with some agreed-upon formula, against counterpart deposits of their own national currencies. They would be held exclusively by the monetary authorities and used only for balance-of-payments settlements, together with gold and in a uniform ratio with it, this ratio being equal to the aggregate ratio of outstanding Fund Units to gold reserves at the time of settlement. Gold and Fund Units would be reshuffled periodically among the participants in order to restore the agreed-upon proportion of Fund Units to gold in the global reserves of each country.[20] Finally, "the counterpart deposits of national currencies would be called upon only in the event of the withdrawal of a member, the liquidation of the system or a decision to cancel part of the outstanding total of CRU's" (paragraph 71).

The final provision just quoted, however, glosses over—to say the least—the crucial revamping of the CRU plan entailed by the experts' later proposal that the counterpart deposits of the developed countries be lent by the Fund

> to the World Bank and its affiliates for investment in the developing countries, receiving IBRD bonds in exchange. This would not alter the total of Fund Units created in the light of the world monetary situation nor to any significant extent the distribution of these Units between developed and developing countries, taken as a whole. But it would mean that each developed country would have to compete for the additional orders for development goods engendered by the World Bank investments, in order to retain the full addition to its reserves represented by the initial distribution of Fund Units. To the extent that each country's share in the additional orders (or, more strictly, in the aggregate trading surplus corresponding to the Bank finance) matched the share of its currency in the Bank loan expenditure, the initial distribution would remain intact; otherwise there would be some re-shuffling of reserves amongst developed countries according to the pattern of excesses and shortfalls between orders secured and currencies contributed. This re-shuffling could affect, of course, only that part of the original reserve creation in respect of which the counterpart currencies were lent to the Bank, and not that part in respect of which the counterpart currencies were retained by the Fund [paragraph 81].

[20] See my article "The Bizarre Proposals of Dr. Bernstein for International Monetary Reform," pp. 333–337.

This proposed link between the creation of reserves needed for monetary purposes, on the one hand, and international development financing, on the other, constitutes to my mind the most valid and significant aspect, by far, of the experts' recommendations. A whole chapter of their report (Chapter IV) is devoted to further clarification of the complex issues involved and to defense of the "propriety" of such a link against traditional and obvious objections, inspired by deep-rooted confusions between the restraint within which an individual banking firm must operate to safeguard its solvency and liquidity, and the totally different criteria that should guide the policies of national monetary authorities and, even more, those of international reserve creation within a worldwide framework.[21]

Far more controversial to my mind—for reasons that will be made clearer in the last section of this book—is the experts' endorsement of the CRU proposal for the initial distribution of Fund Units on the basis of a rigid formula, bearing little or no relation to the actual need for, and usability of, the counterpart deposits to be handed over to the Fund. Among the three alternative formulas mentioned in this respect in the *Ossola Report*, the UNCTAD experts retain the one—that is, the proportionate share of each participating country in the IMF quotas—which would maximize the share allotted to the underdeveloped countries (see Table 6.2). Even then, the share allotted to all the underdeveloped countries, taken together, is no more than 24 percent, of which 9 percent is for Latin America as a whole. If alternative tests, such as "quotas + GAB" or "total reserves" prevailed in fact in the negotiations, these ratios would drop further to about 18 percent and 7 percent, respectively.

This provides a first—even if purely and selfishly nationalistic—reason for the underdeveloped countries not to waste their negotiating ammunition on such a feeble objective, but to direct it instead toward the use of a sizable portion, at least, of counterpart deposits for development financing.

The second reason justifying this strategy, on broader

---

[21] For a fuller discussion, see pp. 137–139 below.

Table 6.2   Alternative Criteria for Distribution of Fund Units
(in percentages of world totals, as of mid-1966)

	Gold	Total Reserves	IMF Quotas	IMF Quotas and GAB
I. Group of Ten	85	72	66	74
A. Reserve centers	38	26	38	41
United States	33	21	26	28
United Kingdom	5	5	12	13
B. European Economic Community	37	33	19	24
C. Other	10	13	9	9
II. Other developed areas	8	12	10	8
III. Less developed areas	7	16	24	18
A. Latin America	2	5	9	7
B. Other	4	11	15	11
IV. World totals	100	100	100	100

grounds, is that the only currencies really useful and usable for this purpose, as well as for the monetary stabilization purposes of the IMF, are those of the surplus countries to which settlements have to be made by the others. The allocation of Fund Units to a country should not be regarded as a privilege, but as compensation for its willingness and ability to transfer real resources to the countries in deficit. The currencies that the Fund should purchase against Fund Units are those that the deficit countries need and of which the Fund is running short: not Brazilian cruzeiros, Argentine pesos, Chilean escudos, Indian rupees, and so on, with which its coffers are already overflowing, but French francs, German marks, Italian lire, Austrian schillings, and so on.

    This is not to say that this situation may not change in the future. On the contrary, the volatility of balances of payments over time assures that it will and that the currencies needed by the Fund tomorrow will not be exactly the same as those it needs today. This is precisely the reason, however, why no rigid formula, such as the relative size of IMF quotas, should serve as a criterion for the distribution of Fund Units. This distribution should adjust instead to the actual needs that will develop over future years, as reflected in the countries' balance of payments, changes in monetary reserves, and net position in the Fund.

7

Convergent Interests
and Operational Solutions

The *Ossola Report* sets forth, most clearly and usefully, the various arguments with which the Group of Ten negotiators justify their opposite answers and solutions to the basic questions on which, in the end, they will have to agree, if the present system is not to drift inexorably toward collapse and chaos.

The same questions will be examined below—although in different order—in the light of the convergent interests of all countries, underdeveloped as well as developed, debtors as well as creditors, in the long overdue readjustment of our haphazard, vulnerable, and outdated international monetary system to the operational requirements of orderly, noninflationary, growth of the world economy. This examination may best be divided into two parts: (1) long-run objectives and solutions, the negotiation of which should not be hurried unduly at the cost of accepting "second-best" compromises for the sake of quick agreement; and (2) the most immediate and less divisive issues on which early agreement is both most urgent and most feasible.

Long-Run Objectives and Solutions

The first, and foremost, of those long-term issues is that which initially prompted the whole debate on international monetary reform, that is, the probable emergence of a future liquidity shortage.

THE AGGREGATE VOLUME OF RESERVE CREATION

A broad consensus has already been reached on the question of the aggregate volume of reserve creation. This consensus, unfortunately, cannot be made fully operational before many other questions relating to its concrete implementation have also been solved to the satisfaction of all participants.

This basic consensus has been aptly summarized in the *1965 Annual Report* of the IMF (p. 15) as a recognition of the need for "the deliberate creation of reserves by collective international action in the light of an appraisal of the general need for reserves rather than on their creation in response to immediate needs of particular countries for balance of payments assistance," and, we might add, as the further haphazard result of gold production, U.S.S.R. gold sales, and speculation on the future rate of exchange between gold and the reserve currencies.

It is further agreed upon that this will involve, at some future stage, the creation of a new type of international reserve asset, supplementing—or replacing—the predominant role assigned today to national reserve currencies, and primarily the dollar, in the process of reserve creation.[1] This need is felt more urgently today by the United States and the United Kingdom, whose gross reserve losses and increasing indebtedness to other countries' central banks have supplied about three fourths of

---

[1] See the *1964 Ministerial Statement of the Group of Ten and Annex Prepared by the Deputies* (referred to below as "The 1964 Group of Ten Report"), paragraph 25 (a), (b), (c), and (d), the *1964 Annual Report* of the IMF, p. 31, and the *1966 Group of Ten Communiqué of Ministers and Governors and Report of Deputies* (referred to below as "The 1966 Group of Ten Report"), paragraphs 7 (b), 29–88, and 46–103.

these countries' total reserve increases over the last fifteen years. The countries of the European Economic Community, on the other hand (whose gross reserves have increased, as a result, by as much as 15 percent a year, on the average, over this fifteen-year period), consider the adoption of any new type of reserve asset as likely to add further inflationary fuel to an already excessive level of reserve creation, as long as it is superimposed upon large and continuing United States and United Kingdom deficits.

The United States and the United Kingdom have agreed with the Europeans (except France) to compromise their differences of view on this issue by initiating immediate "contingency planning" on measures that will be put into actual operation only *if* and *when* needed to combat the deflationary consequences that would follow from a *durable* elimination of the United States and United Kingdom deficits. In the meantime, however, the Europeans have not only ceased to accumulate further dollar and sterling balances as reserves, but have begun to convert massively into gold and gold-guaranteed claims on the Fund some of the dollar and sterling balances accumulated by them in the past.

A different approach would, of course, be far more logical as an answer to the problem and far less dangerous to the stability of the dollar and the pound and of the international monetary system itself. Rather than postpone agreement on deliberate reserve creation until equilibrium in the United States and United Kingdom balances of payments has been achieved and maintained for some unspecified time, the new machinery could be put into place right away, with the understanding that it would be used, *irrespective of United States and United Kingdom deficits or surpluses,* but only (1) automatically—or at least by simple majority decisions—to prevent the actual decline in reserves entailed in the liquidation of *outstanding* dollar and sterling balances by central banks, or private gold purchases in excess of newly available supplies from current production and U.S.S.R. sales; or (2) by qualified vote—two thirds or more of the total voting power—to supplement or replace other sources of reserve increases in the event of a recognized deficiency with relation to needs.

The criteria for the discretionary decisions called forth under (2) are necessarily imprecise, and inseparable, as in the case of national monetary management, from human and fallible judgment. Significant and agreed-upon symptoms of a developing strain and generalized scarcity of reserves are listed in paragraph 10 of the *Ossola Report*.

One need not wait, however, for such developments to forecast confidently large and imperative needs for concerted reserve creation over the long-run future. National money supply will have to grow to sustain feasible growth of production, even in the absence of any inflationary price rises; and international reserves will have to grow both to underwrite such increases in national money stocks in a world of convertible currencies and to cushion temporary disequilibria in expanding levels of world trade.

National money supply—translated into United States dollars as a common unit of measurement—has nearly doubled, over the last fifteen years, for the Group of Ten countries taken together, rising by about 4.7 percent a year, on the average. World imports have risen, over the same period, at an average pace of 6.9 percent a year.[2] The projection of much lower rates of increase than these, let us say 3 percent or 4 percent a year, over the next fifteen years, would require an expansion of $38 billion to $55 billion of the world reserve pool, of which less than $10 billion is likely to become available from new gold production and U.S.S.R. gold sales. The enormity of such figures makes it easier to understand the importance attached by all countries to the rules that will determine their relative influence and voting power in the collective decisions governing the creation, distribution, and uses of reserves in the future.

[2] Exactly equal to the growth rate of international reserves outside the two reserve-center countries whose net reserve losses made such a growth rate compatible with the much lower growth rate of only 2.8 percent a year for world reserves as a whole.

PARTICIPATION AND VOTING RIGHTS

The arguments for and against worldwide membership are summarized in paragraphs 117–122 of the *Ossola Report,* and the weight of opinion within the Group of Ten itself—but obviously not outside it—is fairly reflected in the following conclusion: "Any discrimination in the choice of participants is obviously absurd. But it is also absurd that countries should participate which, because of their past behavior, do not provide adequate guarantees of financial solidity and solvency."[3]

This, again, suggests a limping compromise between opposite viewpoints, calling for a most controversial forecast of future behavior, and separating the sheep from the goats on the basis of an equally controversial appraisal of past performance. A more logical line of approach would recognize that

1. All countries have vital and legitimate interests in the problem and should be associated, in some form, in its solution.

2. Different countries may be called upon, at different times, to grant the international community *immediately effective* claims on their real resources—in the form of balances in their national currency required to settle their current surpluses with the rest of the world—in exchange for *future* claims on other countries' resources—in the form of national reserves usable only to settle their own deficits in the future.

3. The voting power of participating countries in the management of the system must be related, at least in part, to the relative size of their contributions, if these are to be elicited from them on the appropriate, and vast, scale required for the fulfillment of its basic objectives.

[3] This sentence does not appear as such in the pros and cons of the report itself, but on page 84 of a most faithful, lucid, and convenient summary by Mr. Ossola himself, published under the title "On the Creation of New Reserve Assets: the Report of the Study Group of Ten," in the *Banca Nazionale del Lavoro Quarterly Review* (September, 1965), pp. 272–292.

Such an approach would substitute objective and operational criteria for the controversial appraisals and guesswork suggested in the *Ossola Report*. These criteria would be determined essentially by the developing pattern of balances of payments and official settlements between the participating countries. Surplus countries would have to limit their claims to gold settlement to the available supplies, at most, and to accept partial settlement of their claims in the form of the new reserve asset to be created.

This general principle could be implemented in a variety of ways, the simplest of which would be the obligation for each country to keep in the form of IMF reserve deposits an agreed-upon proportion, at least, of either its total reserves or of its future reserve increases, this proportion being determined in the light of the ratio of available gold supplies to the total amount of reserves needed to sustain feasible rates of noninflationary growth in world trade and production. The guidelines presently applied by the Fund in the selection of currencies to be used in drawings and repayments already approximate this result. As pointed out in the *1965 Annual Report* (p. 17),

> the Fund . . . strives to ensure an equitable distribution of reserve positions in the Fund in the light of the balance of payments and reserve positions of the countries whose currencies are considered for drawing. Over the long-run, the reserve positions in the Fund of members whose currencies are suitable for drawing have, as a result of this arrangement, tended to approximate a uniform portion of their total reserves [*emphasis mine*].

This procedure could be simplified, if desired, and extended to all members

1. If the full liquidity and transferability of IMF reserve positions were spelled out in the manner suggested by Governor Ansiaux at the last IMF meeting;[4]

2. And if capital subscriptions to the Fund were dispensed

[4] See pp. 115–116, above.

with, and replaced by the minimum deposit obligations suggested above.

In the meantime, pending such a drastic overhaul of the Fund's machinery, contributions might be called for and accepted, in exchange for IMF reserve positions, only from those countries whose currency threatens to become scarce in the Fund. Such a procedure would be based on Article VII of the present Articles of Agreement and would build on the precedent created by the General Arrangements to Borrow.

RESERVE DEPOSITS WITH THE FUND AS SOURCE OF FUND FINANCING

Reserve deposits would not be created for the purpose of financing credit operations, and their global amounts would be determined in the light of overall reserve requirements rather than of any particular country's or countries' balance-of-payments deficits. They would, however, increase as an inevitable *by-product* the lending capacity of the Fund. How should this lending capacity be used?

It could, of course, be used in normal drawing operations insofar as legitimate and approved needs for such drawings exceed the normal lending capacity of the Fund, derived from the present Articles of Agreement. A special form of this use, extremely important under convertibility conditions, would be that contemplated under the General Arrangements to Borrow, that is, the need to offset through official compensatory financing by the Fund perturbing, but reversible movements of short-term capital between major financial centers. This need might better be served, however, through a reshuffling of the IMF investments to be discussed presently than by the traditional drawing procedures of the Articles of Agreement. Temporary flights of short-term capital from London to New York, for instance, could be offset, in routine manner, by corresponding shifts in the IMF investment assets from United States dollars into pounds sterling, without necessitating a United Kingdom request for drawings susceptible of weakening confidence in the pound.

In the long run, however, a sizable proportion of the Fund's added resources should most usefully be channeled in such a way as to contribute to the financing of the less-developed countries' development needs. Indeed, if Fund lending were to remain constricted—as it has been so far under its normal drawing procedures—to medium-term loans of three to five years' maturity, the gross lending that would prove necessary, year after year, to offset repayments and feed desired increases in world reserves would soon exceed all reasonable needs and uses for such medium-term assistance, while far more urgent needs for longer-term development financing would remain starved for adequate sources of funds.

I am well aware, of course, of the traditional objections to the use of liquid monetary deposits for long-term financing of this sort, either by commercial banks, or even by national central banks. These objections, however, would be totally irrelevant, as brilliantly and wittily shown by Professor Machlup,[5] to the operations of a worldwide reserve center, such as is recommended here. The inflationary dangers of long-term lending—as well as of short-term lending, for that matter—should be adequately guarded against through the limitation of overall reserve creation by the Fund to recognized noninflationary growth needs for reserve increases. Further protection against inflationary abuses by the Fund of its new lending potential could be established by treaty in the form of presumptive ceilings on annual increases of the Fund's outstanding credits, qualified votes of two thirds, four fifths, or more being required to approve increases beyond such ceilings.

As for the danger of illiquidity, usually associated with long-term loans, it could not arise under the proposed system. The world pool of reserves being destined to grow overtime, with little or no probability that circumstances would ever require a sudden

[5] See "The Cloakroom Rule of International Reserves: Reserve Creation and Resources Transfer," *Quarterly Journal of Economics* (August, 1965), p. 343: "For international payments in the same world, the assets (amounts, quality, composition, liquidity) of the international reserve bank (or an appropriately organized IMF) are irrelevant; they become relevant only for payments to persons, banks, or reserve banks on other planets, that is, for *interplanetary* payments."

or massive contraction, the Fund should never have to face any drastic reduction of its deposit liabilities, forcing it to liquidate any substantial portion of its global assets. Balance-of-payments settlements among IMF reserve holders will reshuffle the Fund's deposit liabilities among its members, but should not reduce their total amount.

Yet there exist some valid reasons to limit the maturity of Fund loans and investments. The first is that such limitations will provide added flexibility for shifting the Fund's assistance from some countries to others, whose needs may be greater and which may exceed what the Fund can currently contribute from desirable increases in the total pool of world credit reserves.

A second reason why the Fund should not engage directly in long-term development lending is that such lending requires a very different type of knowledge and expertise than those relevant to its primary tasks and purposes; that is,

1. A rate of creation of overall world reserves most appropriate to sustain noninflationary rates of economic growth;

2. A distribution of its corresponding lending power designed to stimulate the adoption and implementation of desirable readjustment policies by the beneficiaries;

3. The reshuffling of such lending that may be needed to compensate large, but reversible, movements of private capital, particularly among major monetary and financial markets whose general policies are consonant with longer-term equilibrium in their balance of payments.

The bulk of the Fund's assistance to long-term development financing should thus, in all probability, be channeled through—and cushioned by—intermediary institutions specialized in such long-term lending. The Fund might, for instance, distribute its investment portfolio between marketable obligations of international institutions, such as the International Bank for Reconstruction and Development, and other short-term or medium-term investments in the major financial centers— New York, London, Paris, Frankfurt, Amsterdam, and so on —

enabling these to engage more boldly and actively in long-term lending, in the knowledge that temporary pressures on the country's reserves would be offset by a reshuffling of the Fund's own investment portfolio. As already noted before, such reshuffling would be particularly appropriate to meet the objectives now served by the Fund's General Arrangements to Borrow.

PRESSURES FOR BALANCE-OF-PAYMENTS ADJUSTMENT, AND THEIR
  DISTRIBUTION BETWEEN SURPLUS COUNTRIES
  AND DEFICIT COUNTRIES

A recurrent theme of the Group of Ten discussions is the desirability of isolating the process of reserve creation from the financing of balance-of-payments deficits. Reserves should be "earned, owned, unconditional, and to hold" rather than "borrowed, conditional, and to spend."

The first two of these criteria are certainly irreconcilable with the automatic distribution of the new reserve assets to be created among eleven countries, in accordance with some arbitrary formula, and against the assumption of equivalent liabilities—in their national currencies—by the beneficiaries, as advocated in the CRU proposals. CRU's would be neither earned nor fully owned, and would leave the *net* reserves of the group unchanged, increasing gross reserves only *pari passu* with equivalent increases in reserve liabilities.

The only way, indeed, in which net reserves can increase in a form other than gold [6] is through the accumulation of "credit-reserves," that is, of reserve claims entailing international credit operations in one form or another. The suggestions outlined

---

[6] Or other "commodity-reserves," as proposed in a former report to UNCTAD by Hart, Kaldor, and Tinbergen, and in a recent speech of Mendès-France. In order not to lengthen even further an already overlong paper, I have refrained from discussing here a proposal that obviously has no chance to rally agreement or even to be seriously considered in the present negotiations. While superior to a pure gold-reserve system, a commodity-reserve system would seem to me highly wasteful and too blindly automatic, along largely arbitrary lines, to be defensible on economic grounds. This is not to say, however, that some of the Fund lending and investments should not be properly aimed at supporting international efforts to avoid excessive fluctuations in the prices of the major commodities entering international trade.

above would fit far better the very criteria insisted upon by the CRU proponents. While any country might, tomorrow as today, increase its gross reserves through borrowings—from the Fund or other sources—the net reserve claims accumulated on the Fund would have to be "earned" through balance-of-payments surpluses, rather than be received automatically, and would be fully owned and unconditional. Such reserves, moreover, would be accumulated only by countries ready and able to do so and to "hold" them.

It would be absurd, however, to bar countries from "spending" reserves previously earned by them, or even to "borrow" reserves in order to meet temporary balance-of-payments deficits. This is indeed what owned reserves and Fund drawings are for.

As for the "automatic" distribution among eleven countries —or more—of the newly created CRU reserve assets, it would also contravene directly the other cardinal principle, repeatedly emphasized in the Group of Ten discussions; that is, the close interrelationship between the process of adjustment and the need for international liquidity (paragraph 5 of the *1964 Group of Ten Report*), the desirability "to bring under multilateral review and appraisal the various means of financing surpluses or deficits" (paragraph 25 (h)), and the need "for multilateral surveillance of the *various forms of liquidity creation* (italics mine), with a view to avoiding excesses or shortages in the means of financing existing or anticipated surpluses and deficits in the balance of payments, and to discussing measures appropriate for each country in accordance with the general economic outlook" (paragraph 37).

The improvement of the present adjustment mechanism should indeed be an essential objective of the proposed reform, and the distribution of the credits that are the counterpart of any accumulation of fiduciary reserves should be determined in that light rather than by any automatic, and arbitrary, formula. Let us consider separately the nature of the pressures that the present system puts on debtors to eliminate their deficits and on creditors to eliminate their surpluses.

The pressures on the *deficit countries* are obvious enough.

Their ability to finance deficits is limited by the size of their owned reserves and by their access to credit. The owned reserves of deficit-prone countries are, in the vast majority of cases, smaller than might be desirable for the legitimate purpose of offsetting temporary deficits and providing the breathing space needed for the successful working out of the most desirable, but relatively slow-acting, domestic readjustment policies. Access to credit should encourage, but be subordinated to, the adoption and implementation of such policies, as the only alternative to undesirable and unnecessary trade and exchange restrictions and/or devaluation. Currency devaluation may, however, be proved desirable, or even unavoidable, if cost and price disparities have been allowed to develop up to the point where the domestic fiscal and credit policies needed to restore external equilibrium would entail an unacceptable slowdown of employment and production growth.

The financing of even temporary deficits, however, involves some transfer of real resources by the surplus countries to the deficit countries. The overall amount of credit facilities available for this purpose for the world as a whole derives from two sources:

1. The willingness of private and official investors to limit their *immediate* claims on goods and services in exchange for *deferred* claims, through lending and investment operations;

2. The desire of monetary authorities, particularly in the more affluent countries, to earn and accumulate unconditional, owned monetary reserves, in order to retain greater freedom for their own policies in the event of later deficits in their international transactions.

It is this second source that is most directly at stake in the discussion of our present international monetary institutions and in the need for international monetary reform. Conservative estimates of noninflationary requirements for world reserve increases over the next fifteen years range from $38 billion to $74 billion, that is, from $2.5 billion to $5 billion a year, and for fiduciary reserve increases (increases in reserves other than gold metal) from $29 billion to $65 billion, that is, roughly from $2 billion to $4 billion a year. These requirements have been met primarily, under the gold-exchange standard as it has functioned in recent years, by massive and persistent lending to the United States and the United Kingdom by the monetary authorities of other countries. This, in turn, allowed the United States and the United Kingdom to sustain much larger capital exports to other countries—developed, however, as well as underdeveloped—than they would have been able to do otherwise, but at the cost of making themselves increasingly vulnerable to unpredictable conversions into gold of the growing indebtedness accumulated by them, in the process, toward foreign central banks.

The advocacy of a new type of reserve asset derives from the fact that future reserve creation can no longer be fed, on an appropriate scale, by a method involving indefinite increases, by $2 billion a year at the very least, in United States and United Kingdom IOU's, convertible at any time into gold metal. The adoption of a new system of collective, concerted reserve creation should not, however, entail any substantial reduction in the volume of noninflationary requirements for world reserve growth.

Turning now from the deficit countries to the *surplus countries,* it is equally obvious that the present system does not place as stringent limitations on their ability to accumulate large and persistent surpluses as on the ability of the deficit countries to finance large and persistent deficits. It allows any one of them, moreover, to expand, or contract, at will the world reserve pool by deciding unilaterally, at any point in time, on either of two courses:

1. To accept fiduciary reserve assets in settlement of its current surpluses or in exchange of previously accumulated gold reserves;

2. To exact from other countries excessive amounts of limited gold supplies by insisting on gold settlement of its current surpluses, and even of fiduciary reserves accumulated over many years past.

The forthcoming reform of the international monetary system should distribute more equitably and rationally between surplus and deficit countries the burden of balance-of-payments adjustments. The overall pace of reserve creation, or destruction, should be a matter for concerted, collective decisions between all the interested countries. Surplus countries, taken as a group, should be required to accumulate and retain in the form of fiduciary reserve assets the portion of their surpluses that exceeds available gold supplies. Any individual surplus country, however, would retain a free choice between three possible lines of action:

1. To decrease its current-account surpluses by pursuing more expansionary fiscal and monetary policies; or, if this subjects it to undesirable inflationary pressures, by liberalizing its tariff and other import restrictions or, ultimately, by revaluing its exchange rate upward. (The more frequent use of this latter technique would combat the bias toward devaluation—as opposed to revaluation—characteristic of the present system.);

2. To expand its foreign lending, private and/or official;

3. To accumulate fiduciary reserves, with full exchange value and liquidity guarantees, but at correspondingly low rates of interest and in a form susceptible of helping finance the long-term development needs of less-developed countries.[7]

REGIONAL MONETARY INTEGRATION

I doubt whether any negotiable aspect of the proposed reform of the international monetary system is as crucial to the interests of the less-developed countries as the more rational and equitable distribution of balance-of-payments pressures between surplus and deficit countries advocated above (see pp. 139–143). It involves, however, the acceptance of considerable discretion by the Fund authorities in appraising the readjustment policies that deficit countries should follow in order to qualify for Fund assistance.

[7] See pp. 136–139 above.

This, of course, is not new: borrowers—nations as well as individuals—have always had to discuss with the lenders the purposes for which loans are granted and the conditions attached to them. Yet the IMF lending policies have been subject to considerable, and, at times, valid, criticism on this score. Prospective borrowers would undoubtedly welcome some extension of their automatic borrowing rights, as suggested, for example, by Dr. Bernstein, the UNCTAD report, and the IMF itself.

While myself welcoming some move in that direction, I cannot but feel that automatic borrowing rights should be limited to moderate amounts and relatively short maturities, designed to meet unforeseen situations and to provide the time necessary for a deliberate examination of a country's problem and for the reaching of joint agreements on the amounts and purposes of the Fund's assistance. But it would be revolutionary and utopian, indeed, to expect the lenders to accept large automatic commitments to finance blindly the future deficits of all and any country, without regard for the wisdom or folly of the policies that may be at the root of these deficits.

The acceptance of full-fledged discussion with the Fund, as a condition for its assistance, does not involve any surrender of existing national sovereignty. Any country remains free, of course, to reject the Fund's advice, together with the financing facilities subordinated to it. Yet a greater decentralization of the international monetary system, building upon the growing movement toward regional monetary cooperation and integration in many parts of the world, might help avoid unnecessary conflicts between borrowing members and the IMF, and assuage at the same time the objections of prospective surplus countries against surrendering to it full control over the large contributions that they should be called upon to make, in the future, to the required expansion of the world reserve pool.

These contributions would be reduced to a more manageable size if they were designed only to finance disequilibria between each regional group and the rest of the world, and if disequilibria within each group itself were financed from resources contributed to it and on which it retained full control. This is, indeed, the system envisaged for the EEC countries by Article 108 of the Treaty of Rome, and which would be most logically implemented —and probably will be some day—through the creation of the European Reserve Fund, long advocated by Jean Monnet's Action Committee for the United States of Europe.

The Central American countries have already made greater progress in this direction with the establishment of the Central American Clearing House in 1961 (*Cámara de Compensación Centroamericana*) and the 1964 Agreement for the Establishment of the Central American Monetary Union (*Acuerdo para el Establecimiento de la Unión Monetaria Centroamericana*). While more modest in scope, the agreements already concluded among the ALALC countries could serve as a basis for similar cooperation in the future.

The maintenance by each Latin American central bank of an agreed portion of its total reserves in the form of deposits with a central Clearing House would provide the latter with some lending potential enabling it to provide partial assistance at least, even though on a modest and insufficient scale in most cases, to any member in balance-of-payments difficulties. The conditions attached to such lending would be discussed among the Latin American countries themselves, and might be more realistically conceived than those imposed at times by the IMF Executive Board. If a further approach to the Fund proved nec-essary—as would undoubtedly often be the case—to supplement the scant resources of the Latin American Clearing House, it could take the form of a "concerted action" by all members, as foreseen in Article 108, 2(a) of the Rome Treaty. Such support would carry all the more weight, as it would have been under-written in advance by other members' willingness to commit their own resources to the support of the readjustment policies of the borrowing country.

If, on the other hand, the policies of the prospective bor-rower were deemed inadequate by its Latin American partners to justify their own financial assistance, they could not then blame the IMF for insisting also on further policy action as a condition for its own lending.[8]

An Urgent First Step

The solution of the long-run problems discussed above—the adjustment of reserve creation to the monetary requirements of economic growth, and the use of the resulting lending potential to reinforce desirable pressures for adjustment on both surplus and deficit countries—will exercise a crucial influence, for better or for worse, on the future of our world, for many years to come.

ARGUMENTS FOR NEGOTIATING PRIORITY

They are also problems, however, that still raise complex and divisive issues among the negotiators, in view of opposite economic, political, and emotional reactions regarding the desirable pace and legitimate purposes of reserve increases, the role of

[8] For further discussion of these issues and of alternative methods for implementation, see:

"Intégration economique et politique monétaire," *La Restauration des monnaies européennes* (special issue of the *Revue d'Economie Politique*, Sirey, Paris: December, 1960), pp. 58–81, translated as "Integración económica europea y política monetaria," *Coordinación Monetaria Regional,* CEMLA (1963), pp. 43–63; *La Communauté Économique Européenne et la coopération monétaire internationale* (report to the Xth Round Table on Europe's Problems, Basle, November, 1962), reproduced in *Problèmes de l'Europe* (1963); "Una cámara de compensación y union de pagos latinoamericana," *Cooperación Financiera en América Latina,* CEMLA (1963), pp. 95–117; "Hacia una organización monetaria latino-americana," *La Integración de América Latina: Experiencias y Perspectivas,* Miguel Wionczek, ed. (Mexico and Buenos Aires: Fondo de Cultura, 1964); "International Monetary Arrangements, Capital Markets, and Economic Integration in Latin America," *Journal of Common Market Studies* (1965); translated as "Acuerdos monetarios internacionales, mercados de capital e integración económica de América Latina," *Revista de Economia Latinoamericana* (1964); *Report on the Possibilities of Establishing a Clearing and Payments Union in Africa,* United Nations Economic and Social Council, E/CN. 14/262, February 4, 1964; "Payments Arrangements within the ECAFE Region" (to be published in late 1967 by ECAFE); and "The Contribution of Regional Monetary Integration to World-Wide Monetary Reform" (discussed at a Colloquium on the Impact of Regional Economic Groupings on East-West Relations, Budapest, September 10–14, 1967; to be published in *Acta Oeconomica,* Budapest, in 1967 or early 1968).

gold in the system, the necessary surrenders, or rather mergers, of national monetary sovereignty that may be required, the selection of countries that should participate in these decisions, their relative voting power, the degree of automaticity that might prove acceptable as an alternative to continuous negotiations in cases of disagreement, and so on. Any practical reconciliation of views of these matters is most likely to require considerable time still. Undue haste in reaching agreement would most probably entail undesirable compromises centering on the lowest, rather than the highest, common denominator between the opposite objectives and techniques now favored by the major reserve debtors and reserve creditors of the Group of Ten.[9]

The major reserve holders of continental Europe, without whom an optimum agreement on these long-term issues remains impossible, continue to view with suspicion any discussion of concerted reserve increases that might be used to underwrite in advance future international rescue operations in favor of the reserve currencies, whenever their central banks refuse to add further amounts of dollar and sterling IOU's to holdings that they deem already far in excess of their requirements.

The removal of this obstacle to a negotiated agreement depends primarily on the United States and the United Kingdom, on the one hand, and the major reserve holders of continental Europe, on the other, rather than on any action that could be undertaken by the less-developed countries. Yet, any agreement that could be reached to protect the dollar and the pound against unnecessary devaluation would also be of major interest to them, since they hold in fact most of their monetary reserves in the

---

[9] The danger of some such undesirable compromise looms larger indeed, as this manuscript goes to press, and adds to the urgency of a more active and forceful participation by the less-developed countries in the forthcoming IMF debate. The major issue at stake is the link between reserve creation and development financing (see pp. 126–127 and 137–139 above) advocated by UNCTAD, but strongly opposed so far by the Group of Ten. Support for such a "link" may be building up in the United States Congress. See the recent report to the Joint Economic Committee by Representatives Henry S. Reuss (chairman of the Subcommittee on International Exchange and Payments) and Robert F. Ellsworth, *Off Dead Center: Some Proposals to Strengthen Free World Economic Cooperation* (Washington, D.C.: December, 1965).

form of dollar and sterling balances. Moreover, concrete agreement on ways and means to *expand* reserves, when needed, in the most rational and efficient manner, would be greatly facilitated if a machinery had already been established previously—along the lines suggested below—to prevent their contraction.

Such an agreement should be given the highest priority in the current negotiations, as it is both far more urgent and should prove far easier to negotiate rapidly, than measures aiming at future reserve increases.

It is more urgent in view of the large mass of foreign-exchange reserves (about $22 billion) legally convertible at any time into gold metal by their holders, directly or indirectly. Such conversions could be triggered by political, as well as strictly economic, developments: fears of blocking, refusal to ease the financing of the debtor countries' deficits, fears of a change in gold parities, and so on. *The liquidation of $3.2 billion of foreign-exchange reserve assets by developed countries other than the United States and the United Kingdom in the first six months of 1965 only (see pp. 99–102 above) and another billion dollars in the following twelve months testifies to the reality of this danger.*

Such measures should also be far easier to negotiate, as they do not require any reconciliation of views about the desirable pace of reserve increases, the geographical distribution of such increases, the policies that they would support, and so on. All that is involved is the necessity of avoiding any massive contraction of already outstanding foreign-exchange claims and debts accumulated over many years past and long incorporated into the existing structure of world reserves.[10]

BROAD FEATURES OF PROPOSED INITIAL AGREEMENT

Eight countries (the United States, the United Kingdom, Switzerland, France, Germany, Italy, Belgium, and the Netherlands) have traditionally long held a much larger proportion of their total monetary reserves in gold metal than have other countries. As of June, 1966, for instance, gold accounted for 75 percent, and

---

[10] For a more detailed discussion of negotiability, see the section "Negotiability of Such an Agreement" below, pp. 152–156.

foreign exchange for only 16 percent, of their total reserves (the remaining 9 percent being held in claims on the IMF). In contrast, other countries held only 30 percent of their reserves in gold but as much as 62 percent in foreign exchange. The gold holdings of these eight countries accounted, as of the same date, for more than four fifths of the total for all the countries in the world outside the communist bloc.

These different preferences, as between sterile gold holdings and interest-earning reserve balances in foreign currencies, are

Table 7.1   Reserve Composition, 1937–June 1967

	1937	1949	1959	1964	June, 1967
A. Percentage of world gold held by					
1. Eight countries	88	87	84	82	81
2. All other countries	12	13	16	18	19
B. Percentage of gold in reserves of					
1. Eight countries	99	90	82	76	74
2. All other countries	58	33	32	30	29
C. Percentage of foreign exchange in reserves of					
1. Eight countries	1	5	11	17	18
2. All other countries	42	66	65	65	64

SOURCE: *International Financial Statistics.*

traditional ones (see Table 7.1) and are easily explainable by the following three sets of considerations:

1. A greater concern of what we might term the "gold bloc" countries for political autonomy: Gold reserves were often regarded as a "war chest," the German Empire, for instance, holding a portion of them separately in the Spandau Fortress rather than in the Reichsbank.

2. The greater urge of less affluent countries for the interest earnings derived from foreign-exchange holdings.

3. The fact that a large portion of the latter countries' reserves are derived from borrowings—many of them short term—in New York and London, and dependent on the maintenance of dollar and sterling balances in these two money centers. The short-term indebtedness of non-European countries to the United States at the end of 1965 ($8 billion) exceeded in fact their total official dollar holdings ($6.7 billion).

Future compatibility between global demand and supply of monetary gold, at present gold prices, is crucially dependent on concerted action by the first group of countries, limiting their total demand for gold to available supplies. Any agreement of this sort, however, would clearly be unnegotiable at the present juncture, if it implied the obligation for the six continental European countries to accumulate and retain in the currencies of the other two (the United Kingdom and the United States) all or most of any future accruals to their present monetary reserves. This would hardly be in the interests of the underdeveloped countries themselves and would clash directly with the "multilateral surveillance" principle repeatedly affirmed in the *1964 Group of Ten Report,* since it would earmark quasi-automatically the largest portion of prospective reserve accumulation for loans—required or unrequired—to the United States and the United Kingdom.

If this is to be avoided, and if the use of the lending counterpart of reserve accumulation is to be brought under multilateral surveillance, reserve holders should be provided with an alternative reserve asset, sufficiently safe and attractive to serve as a substitute for gold itself as well as for dollars and sterling.

The agreement outlined at the end of this chapter would set up for this purpose a Gold Conversion Account, administered jointly by the participating countries. Each of these would deposit with this Gold Conversion Account any excess of foreign-currency balances accumulated by its monetary authority over and above normal working balances needed for stabilization interventions in the exchange markets and anticipated needs for debt repayments to the country (or countries) in the currency of which such balances are held.

Deposits with the Gold Conversion Account would carry full gold-value guarantees[11] and a modest rate of interest. They would be used primarily and on sight (or short notice) to replenish depleted working balances in any participating currency. They could, moreover, also be converted at any time into gold metal by any depositor whose ratio of such deposits to total reserves is higher than the average ratio for the participating countries taken together. Conversely, the countries whose deposit ratio is the lowest would agree to raise it by transferring gold to their Account. These transfers would be made to the extent necessary to meet the actual gold withdrawals of other members.

Future currency balances accruing to any country and turned over by it to the Account would be automatically and immediately repayable in gold to the Account by the debtor countries insofar as they exceeded the foreign-currency balances turned over by these countries themselves to the Account. This rule, however, would not be applied to the currency balances already *outstanding* at the time the agreement entered into force and accumulated over long years of functioning of the present gold-exchange standard. Indeed, one of the primary purposes of the agreement would be to guard against the sudden and immediate contraction of the world reserve pool, the unsustainable gold losses by the reserve-currency countries, and the consequent threat of collapse of the international monetary system, which such conversions might entail. The *outstanding* currency balances *initially* transferred to the Account would therefore be retained by it, subject to agreement with the debtors on full gold-value guarantees and modest interest payments. They would be gradually amortized over a period of years:

[11] Other guarantees against default, blocking, and so on, are spelled out in my paper "The International Monetary System," *Moorgate and Wall Street* (Summer, 1965), pp. 33–34, reprinted in *Guidelines for International Monetary Reform* (Hearings before the Subcommittee on International Exchange and Payments of the Joint Economic Committee of Congress, Washington, D.C.: 1965), Part 2: Supplement, pp. 358–359, and in my book *The World Money Maze* (New Haven, Conn.: Yale University Press, 1966), pp. 346–372.

1. As a minimum, to reduce excessive demands by the debtors for conversion into gold of the surpluses accumulated by them in the future;

2. If needed to reach agreement, by periodic installments, at a rate not exceeding 2 or 3 percent a year, such contractual amortization to be postponed, however, whenever deemed in conflict with the general stabilization objectives of the IMF.

NEGOTIABILITY OF SUCH AN AGREEMENT

The last column of Table 7.2 shows the *maximum* amounts of gold reshufflings that might have been entailed by the proposed agreement, if it had come into operation as of September 30, 1966. While a different date would, of course, modify these estimates, they can be used nevertheless as a rough indication of the magnitudes involved and of the privileges and commitments entailed for the prospective participants.

Acceptability to the Reserve-Currency Creditors of Continental Europe. The reserve-currency creditors of continental Europe (that is, Switzerland and the EEC countries), taken as a group, would limit to about $0.7 billion theoretical gold-conversion rights totaling, as of September 30, 1966, more than $5 billion (see the fourth and fifth lines of columns f and b, respectively, of Table 7.2). This would leave most of them free to convert into gold, if they wished, substantial amounts of foreign-exchange reserves (up to nearly $0.9 billion in the case of Germany). Only three countries (France, Switzerland, and the Netherlands) might be forced to sell minor amounts of their gold holdings to the Account, and this only in the very unlikely case in which the first countries all used to the full their gold-conversion rights.

The availability of both interest earnings and full guarantees against devaluation, default, blocking, and so on, on these new Gold Account deposits would hardly induce massive conversions of such deposits into gold metal by countries that previously refrained from converting into gold unguaranteed foreign-exchange assets exposed to all these risks. Actual conversions into gold would, therefore, be most likely to remain well below the maximum figures shown in column f of Table 7.2. In the

Table 7.2 **Maximum Impact of Proposed Gold Conversion Account Agreement upon Direct Gold Holdings of Members**
(in millions of United States dollars, as of September 30, 1966)

	Gross Reserves (a)	Foreign Exchange Component (b)	Assumed Working Balances (c = 5% of a)	Maximum Calls for Gold Conversion Deposits		Gold Deposit (−) or Withdrawal Rights (+) (f = e − d)
				Total (d = 11.4% of a)	From Excess Foreign Exchange (e = b − c)	
I. Reserve centers	18040	2270	900	2060	1370	−690
United States	14880	1150	740	1700	410	−1290
United Kingdom	3160	1120	160	360	960	+600
II. Switzerland	2830	250	150	330	100	−230
III. European Community	23840	4840	1190	2720	3650	+920
France	6880	650	340	790	310	−480
Netherlands	2410	270	120	280	150	−130
Belgium	2290	400	120	260	280	+20
Germany	7670	2160	380	880	1780	+900
Italy	4590	1360	230	520	1130	+610
Total	44810	7360	2240	5120	5120	0
Group average percentage of gross reserves	100	16.4	5	11.4	11.4	0

NOTES:

1. Needed working balances (column c) are arbitrarily assumed, for concreteness' sake, to fluctuate between 0 percent and 10 percent, and to average 5 percent of gross reserves.

2. "Excess" foreign-exchange balances (column e) are then measured by the excess of column b over column c; for the eight countries taken together, such "excess foreign-exchange balances" ($5.1 billion) average about 11.4 percent of gross reserves ($44.8 billion).

3. Column d applies this proportion uniformly to each country's gross reserves to determine the deposit obligation that it might, at the limit, be required to hold with the Account if all participants used to the fullest possible extent their rights to gold conversions (column d = 11.4 percent of column a).

4. Finally, column f shows the maximum amount of gold that each country might be called upon, under that extreme hypothesis, to transfer to the Account in order to complete its minimum deposit (minus signs), or would have the right to draw from the account (plus signs), as of September 30, 1966 (column f = column e − column d).

course of time, after sufficient experience had been gained with the new system, one should even expect opposite shifts to take place, that is, to have participating countries sell gold voluntarily to the Account in exchange for gold-guaranteed and interest-earning Gold Account deposits, as freely usable as gold itself for balance-of-payments settlements.

Acceptability to the Reserve-Currency Debtors. The United Kingdom's foreign-exchange reserves were substantially larger, as of September 30, 1966, than the amounts that it might be required, even at the limit, to hold with the Account under the proposed agreement. Its position was, therefore, in this respect, similar to that of the majority of the continental European participants discussed above: it would have the right to withdraw gold, rather than be obliged to deposit gold with the Account.

The United States, on the other hand, would expose itself to gold conversions totaling, as a maximum, about $1300 million,[12] but likely to be far smaller in fact—or even nil—for the reasons brought forth above (pp. 152–154). It would also, however, be fully guaranteed against the much larger gold conversions that the other seven participating countries might legally exact from it today or tomorrow, either in anticipation of a revaluation of gold, or because of their refusal to participate in the financing of United States deficits and policies with which they disagree, or as a bludgeoning weapon to force the United States to change such policies, or in order to protect themselves against possible United States blocking of their dollar accounts in the extreme case of more acute political divergences, and so on.

This is only one of the reasons why the United States should regard such an agreement as of major benefit to itself, independently of its interest in the other, and broader, objectives of international monetary reform. Another reason is the fact that the consequent abatement of any expectation of a forced revaluation

[12] In view of the guarantees attached to the Gold Account deposits that the United States would require in exchange, these could properly continue to be regarded as part of the United States gold reserves, just as no deduction is now made from them for the amounts due to foreign or international monetary authorities, even when these entail a full gold commitment (as is the case, for example, for the $800 million of IMF gold invested in United States securities).

of gold, as a result of massive dollar conversions by the increasingly reluctant holders of continental Europe, would almost certainly induce a spectacular reversal in gold and currency speculation, which is probably responsible today for most, or all, of the
residual deficits in the United States balance of payments. Hoarding and speculative gold purchases, not accounted for by industrial and artistic uses, more than doubled following the gold
flare-up of October, 1960, and were running in 1965 at about
three times their average amounts in the decade of the 1950's.
Speculative gold stocks have thus risen by a total amount of $6
billion, or more, in the last seven years alone. An agreement—
such as suggested here—making both obvious and operational
the determination of the major gold-holding countries to avoid
any change in gold prices would undoubtedly dishearten the gold
speculators and induce them to unload several billions of the
enormous and costly gold hoards accumulated by them in an-
ticipation of a proximate revaluation of the price of gold. The
funds released by such dishoarding would have to be reinvested,
and the largest portion of them would have to seek such rein-
vestment in the major financial markets of the world, that is, in
New York, and even London, thus reversing the heavy flights of
short-term capital to which these countries have been exposed in
recent years.

The overall deficits of the United States balance of payments
were, until the escalation of the Vietnam war, far smaller
than the $2.6 billion reversal in average yearly short-term capital
movements experienced by our country, beginning with the
spread of revaluation rumors in 1960, and which replaced about
$1 billion a year of normal *inflows* toward a major financial center
in the late 1950's (1955–1959) with abnormal *outflows* of $1.6
billion a year in the first half of the 1960's (1960–1964).[13]

Two possible United States objections to the proposed agreement require a final word of comment.

[13] A more sophisticated econometric study of Jerome L. Stein similarly estimates
at about $2.5 billion a year the impact of speculative capital movements on the
United States balance of payments in the absence of interest-rate differentials.
See his "International Short-Term Capital Movements," *American Economic
Review* (March, 1965), pp. 40–66.

The first is the cost of the gold-value guarantee on the short-term dollar balances initially transferred to the Account and consolidated by it into long-term obligations. Such a guarantee would, of course, be a prerequisite for such consolidation, but it should prove costless in fact, if it helps us honor our repeatedly reiterated pledge to maintain the stability of the dollar, by removing a major threat to our ability to do so. We would, moreover, effect right away substantial savings on the balances so transferred, since interest costs would be far lower on such gold-guaranteed obligations than on present unguaranteed dollar balances.

The second objection is that we would have to give up the expectation of having our future deficits financed in large part and quasi-automatically by further piling up of dollar balances as reserves by the participating countries. Such an expectation, however, would hardly seem realistic at this stage, and its abandonment would be a small price to pay for the protection gained against far more likely conversions into gold of our *outstanding* indebtedness to them. It would, moreover, clash head-on with the "multilateral surveillance" principle under which such financing should be subject to multilateral consultation and remain available to us, on a vast scale indeed, through the IMF, the General Arrangements to Borrow, and the further provisions that might expand, in a second stage of negotiations, the functions of the Gold Conversion Account itself (see under "Link to Long-Term Objectives," pp. 158–160 below). In any case, our present *gross* reserve assets—equivalent to about 65 percent of annual imports —should amply cover any legitimate needs for future deficit financing, if they could be earmarked for this purpose alone and protected against sudden or massive liquidation of our most vulnerable reserve liabilities.

EXTENSION TO OTHER COUNTRIES

The adoption of the proposed agreement by the eight countries listed above would, in itself, benefit all other countries—with the chief exception of South Africa, of course—by removing one of the main and most immediate threats to the stability of the currency in which they hold the bulk of their reserves and, as a consequence, to the stability of the international monetary system itself.

Yet other countries might wish to join the Agreement, and the accession of some of them at least would be highly desirable to enlarge the scope of multilateral surveillance.

The main difficulty to be faced arises from the fact that the accession of many other countries, on similar terms, might lead to a substantial lowering of the minimum gold ratio that could be guaranteed to members. As long as the eight initial members of the Agreement retain their traditional attachment to gold reserves, they might resist the dilution of their gold ratio that might be entailed by the accession of other countries to the system.

This obstacle would become weaker, however, and should indeed be totally overcome in time if, as foreseen above, familiarity with the advantages of Gold Account deposits gradually induces a preference for them as a more attractive medium than sterile gold hoards for reserve holding.

In the meantime, it could be overcome through the negotiation of separate agreements regarding the maximum use that a new member might wish, or be able, to make of its gold-conversion rights, particularly with regard to its already outstanding foreign-currency reserves. Both desire and ability to request such conversions would be far lower in any case than might be suggested by the estimates reported in columns b and e of Table 7.2:

1. Because the global reserves of most countries other than the initial signatories are far closer to minimum working levels, needed for interventions in the market, and leave therefore relatively little room for conversion into Gold Account deposits;

2. Because a substantial portion of these reserves is derived from relatively short-term borrowings in New York or London, which might not be renewed if their central banks decreased their deposits in these centers;

3. Because preference for gold is traditionally much weaker in most of these countries, and more than offset by their desire to maximize earnings (available from foreign-exchange

reserves and, at a much lower rate, from Gold Account deposits, but not from gold reserves);

4. In the case of the so-called sterling area, because of somewhat more formal arrangements inducing the overseas sterling members to retain a large portion of their reserves in the form of sterling balances in London.

Finally, the abatement of gold revaluation fears and the gold-value guarantees offered on Gold Account deposits would also contribute to decreasing even further the likelihood of any sudden and irrational desire for gold, on the part of countries in which the gold thirst is not deeply rooted in past habits, routines, and tradition. In the latter case, even more than in the case of Europe, one might expect opposite shifts from sterile gold hoards into voluntarily held Gold Account deposits.

LINK TO LONG-TERM OBJECTIVES

The implementation of the initial Agreement suggested above would not solve, admittedly, the long-run problem of providing for adequate reserve increases in an expanding world economy. It would, however, facilitate later negotiation of the measures required for this purpose and that could, most easily and logically, be grafted upon the machinery put in place to guard against the threat of a sudden decline in already existing reserve levels.

Three such lines of development may be mentioned briefly here, even though it would be wise to postpone such "contingency planning" until the problem becomes actual, and evident to all, and sufficient confidence has been built in the new Gold Conversion Account deposits as a safe, liquid, and highly attractive medium for reserve accumulation by central banks.

1. One possibility is the integration of the GAB into the Gold Conversion Account Agreement. Whenever circumstances arose under which the participating countries would agree to resort to the present GAB provisions, they could instead direct the Gold Conversion Account to invest an appropriate portion of its gold assets in gold-guaranteed obli-

gations of the country requesting an exchange transaction or standby arrangement "necessary in order to forestall or cope with an impairment of the international monetary system . . . in the new conditions of widespread convertibility, including greater freedom for short-term capital movements. . . ." (GAB, paragraph 6 and Preamble).

The increasing preference of members for Gold Account deposits rather than gold-metal reserves should provide ample resources for such operations. If, however, and to the extent that the gold resources of the account might become inadequate for this purpose, recourse would be taken to paragraph 6 of the proposed Gold Conversion Account Agreement, preferably under the more flexible voting provisions suggested for the operation of the latter. (It might still be possible, if no agreement on voting rules could be reached otherwise, to recognize the right of minority countries to abstain from participation in an operation decided by majority vote. Only the majority countries would, in that case, agree to raise the proportion of their total reserves to be held in the form of deposits with the Gold Conversion Account.)

2. Exactly the same procedures set forth immediately above could be used whenever the participating countries agreed on the *need to increase world reserves* by any given amount.

I myself have long argued that such a decision might then best be carried out through investments in IBRD obligations or in gold-guaranteed obligations of the countries most able and willing to engage in long-term financing of the development needs of the underdeveloped areas of the world (see pp. 136–139 above). This, after all, is the only way in which the richer industrial countries could increase their "earned" *net* reserves, as opposed to "mutually borrowed" *gross* reserves. Official opinion, in continental Europe at least, still seems to incline toward other and more automatic solutions, distributing the new reserve assets pro rata of each country's gold holdings, or IMF quotas, or other predetermined criteria. To my mind, this would be incompatible with their repeatedly asserted objective of linking increases in world reserves to the improvement of the present balance-of-payments adjustment mechanism and policies.

In any case, I see no reason to try to force an immediate, once-and-for-all resolution of these conflicting views in favor of a single formula. The choice between the above alternatives—and indeed others—could be left to the *ad hoc* decision of the participating countries at the time when they agree on need for a reserve increase, and might differ with each individual case, in the light of prevailing conditions and major policy objectives at that time. Whatever reserve increase is then deemed desirable could be implemented in a variety of ways, including not only those briefly summarized above, but also, for instance, Gold Conversion Account gold or currency deposits with the IMF designed to enlarge the capacity of the Fund to finance normal drawings under the Articles of Agreement.

3. A third possible use of Gold Conversion Account investments might occasionally arise in connection with the repayment of IMF drawings at the end of the maximum three-to-five-year period specified in the Executive Board's decisions of February 13, 1952, and December 23, 1953. Circumstances might arise under which such repayment might be deemed undesirable, both from the point of view of the country concerned, in the light of its circumstances and policies at the time, and from the point of view of the evolution of world reserves themselves. The members of the Gold Conversion Account might then deem it appropriate to offset the unwanted impact of such repayment through investments in the obligations of the repaying country. Such investments would not, by themselves, lead to any new increases, but merely avoid a decline in the outstanding level of world reserves.

(Such a procedure might, for instance, prove useful to smooth out over a longer period of time the large IMF repayment obligations of Britain, in view of the extremely low and inadequate reserve levels of that country.)

ON THE RELATION OF THE ABOVE PROPOSALS TO OTHER CURRENT
PROPOSALS FOR INTERNATIONAL MONETARY REFORM

The proposals above combine into a single package various suggestions made in the past by the negotiators of the Group of Ten, and particularly:

1. Robert V. Roosa's suggestion for a less asymmetrical system of assuring the convertibility of the major currencies used in world trade. Only the United States and France now redeem directly into gold metal excess holdings of their currencies presented for conversion by central banks. This, however, is due to the fact that these two countries hold the bulk of their monetary reserves in gold, and relatively little in foreign exchange. If other countries were to be asked to redeem their currency in gold—rather than as now in dollars—this might induce them to convert much of their present dollars into gold. This is obviously not what Mr. Roosa wants.

My alternative suggestion for a Gold Conversion Account would restore full symmetry between all participating currencies with respect to their conversion rights and obligations, without entailing massive losses of gold by the present reserve-currency countries.

2. French, German, and Dutch suggestions for a more harmonious and equitable distribution of gross reserves between gold and foreign currencies.

3. Belgian suggestions aiming at making fully liquid—and thus acceptable as monetary reserves for central banks—international assets other than gold metal alone.

4. Italian and other suggestions (from Mr. Roosa, for instance) for applying this technique to the consolidation of the excessive short-term indebtedness of Britain, while preserving the liquidity of such claims.

5. French suggestions to base such assets upon adequate gold-value and gold-convertibility guarantees.

6. Former Chancellor Maudling's plan, with three modifications designed to (a) mop up *ex ante,* rather than *ex post,* unrequired foreign-currency reserves whose sudden unloading may at any time trigger crises for the debtor country, (b) ensure the full acceptability and transferability of his "mutual currency accounts," and (c) clarify the repayment obligations of the debtor countries.

7. The IMF proposals for Fund investments, decided at the initiation of the Fund, and financed by members' reserve deposits.

APPENDIX TO CHAPTER 7:

PROPOSED INITIAL AGREEMENT FOR THE ESTABLISHMENT OF A GOLD CONVERSION ACCOUNT AMONG MAJOR GOLD RESERVE HOLDERS

1. Belgium, France, Germany, Italy, the Netherlands, Switzerland, the United Kingdom, and the United States will establish and administer jointly a "Gold Conversion Account," using the IMF (or the BIS?) as Agent.

2. Each participating country will deposit with this Gold Conversion Account any excess of foreign-currency balances accumulated by its monetary authorities over and above working balances needed for stabilization interventions in the exchange markets and anticipated needs for debt repayments to the country (or countries) in the currency of which such balances are held.

(It might be deemed desirable to specify maximum ceilings on retained holdings, in order to implement the "multilateral surveillance" objective affirmed in the report of the Group of Ten, and to avoid excessive monetary financing, by unilateral decisions or bilateral negotiations, of any participating country's deficits, susceptible of imposing unwanted inflationary pressures on other countries.)

3. Deposits with the Gold Conversion Account will carry full gold-value guarantees and a modest rate of interest. They will be used primarily and on sight (or short notice) to replenish depleted working balances in any participating currency, but may also be withdrawn at any time in gold metal by the depositor, subject to provisions 6, b, (ii), and (iii) below.

4. Outstanding currency balances initially transferred to the Account will be retained by it, subject to agreement with the debtor on full gold-value guarantees and modest interest payments. They will be subject to:

a. regular amortization at a rate not exceeding (2, 3, or 5?) percent a year, such amortization to be postponed, however, whenever deemed in conflict with the general stabilization objectives of the IMF;

b. extraordinary amortization under provision 6, b (ii) below.

5. Other currency balances subsequently transferred to the Account will be automatically repayable by the debtors, either through their own transfers to the Account of other participating countries' currencies accruing to them, or in gold.

6. Any global imbalance between gold payments to and gold withdrawals from the Account[14] will be dealt with in the following manner:

a. In the event of gold accumulation in the Account deemed excessive by the participating countries, interest rates may be lowered on its deposit liabilities.

b. If a shortage of gold threatens to develop in the Account:

i. interest rates may be raised on its deposit liabilities;

ii. demands for gold withdrawals by countries indebted to the Account (as a result of provision 4 above) may be met instead by extraordinary amortization of their outstanding indebtedness;

iii. if the above measures prove insufficient to deal with a threatening gold shortage in the Account, the countries whose ratio of Account deposits to total reserves is lowest will agree to raise it by selling gold to the Account to the extent necessary to meet the gold withdrawals of other members. (This would tend to diminish the present spread in reserve composition and might, as a limiting case, ul-

---

[14] Such imbalance might arise only as a result of provision 4 above concerning the outstanding currency balances initially transferred to, and retained by, the Account. Provision 5 would automatically exclude any gold imbalance with respect to subsequent operations, unless and until the initial agreement were modified in accordance with provision 9 below.

timately adjust such composition on the eight countries' average.)

7. Any other convertible-currency country may be invited to participate, provided that:

a. it accepts the obligations specified above;

b. it agrees not to use the gold-conversion right specified under provision 3 above to increase its holdings of gold metal beyond its traditional ratio to total reserves. (Such "traditional" ratio would have to be agreed upon, before accession, and might be calculated on the basis of a past reference period as well as other factors, such as the country's offsetting indebtedness in the currency in which a large portion of its total monetary reserves are customarily held.)

8. The pattern of voting rights to be agreed upon should be based largely (or even exclusively?) on the relative size of each participating country's average deposits and contingent commitments under provision 6, b (iii) above. [At the limit, a voting pattern determined by commitments alone (see column d of Table 7.2, p. 153 above) would just about equilibrate initially the combined voting power of the United States, the United Kingdom, and Switzerland with that of the five EEC participants. The actual pattern would vary, however, in the course of time, with changes in each country's total reserves and commitments and in any additional free deposits with the Account.]

9. *Contingency Planning:* Whenever the participating countries agree on the need to protect the international monetary system against either (a) a worldwide shortage of international reserve media, or (b) the impact of speculative shifts of short-term funds between major money markets in the conditions specified in the Preamble to the General Arrangements to Borrow, they will:

a. direct the Account to invest to that effect an agreed portion of its assets in specified international or national obligations of the highest standing and carrying a gold-value guarantee;

b. increase to the extent necessary the deposits which they may be called upon to retain with the Account under Provision 6, b (iii) above.

8

Summary

and Conclusions

Man's future evolves inevitably from his past. The future evolution of the international monetary system will similarly bear the marks of past and current history.

The Evolution of National Monetary Systems from Commodity Moneys to Fiduciary Money

Money has progressively evolved, all over the world, from early "commodity moneys" (such as gold and silver) toward "fiduciary money" (currency and deposits). Commodity money was not, however, displaced overnight by fiduciary money. Both coexisted for more than a century and remained convertible into one another at the discretion of their holders.

The slow displacement of commodity money by fiduciary money was, however, practically completed when World War I erupted and accelerated the process. The last vestiges of commodity money disappeared throughout most of the world in the 1920's, and in the United States in 1933.

The ease with which fiduciary money could be created by the issuing institutions, but also destroyed through its conversion into scarcer commodity money, exposed the process to excessive, inflationary money creation, followed by deflationary contraction, financial crises, and banking collapses. This prompted everywhere the emergence and development of central banks, backed by the political authority of the state, and charged with the task of orienting and underwriting the creation of fiduciary money in such a way as to avoid such crises.

The state gradually conferred on these central banks an exclusive monopoly over the issue of currency notes and made these "legal tender" in the discharge of all debts, public and private. This, in turn, enabled these central banks to assume the responsibilities of "lender of last resort" and to provide temporary financial assistance to deposit banks when the latter encountered difficulties by reason of their obligation to convert their own deposit liabilities into legal-tender money.

Central banks normally became, for this reason, the main depositories of the deposit banks' cash reserves, which previously had been held in part with other deposit banks and exposed the latter to heavier deposit withdrawals susceptible of triggering successive banking collapses and panics in times of stress. This autonomous trend toward a single reserve system was later formalized in a number of countries, beginning with the United States, by legislation on minimum-deposit requirements. Such legislation was used later as a further instrument for the orientation and control of deposit-money creation.

The growing safety and popular acceptance of fiduciary reserves and fiduciary money enabled the national monetary systems to adjust money supply to the requirements of expanding trade and production levels, and to escape the constraints otherwise imposed upon the process by erratic fluctuations and/or shortages in the production of the monetary metals; that is, silver and gold initially, but primarily gold alone in the heyday of the gold standard.

Fiduciary money, however, circulated only within each country's borders. The preservation of an *international* payments system thus came to depend increasingly upon the continued convertibility of *national* fiduciary money into *international* commodity money; that is, gold, after silver coins themselves became fiduciary money when the international price of silver as a commodity was allowed to drop below its nominal value in the last third of the nineteenth century.

Responsibility for such convertibility of *national* fiduciary moneys into *international* commodity money devolved upon the issuers of legal tender; that is, upon the central banks. While every other firm or individual could discharge its debts by "tendering" to its creditors legal-tender fiduciary money, the central banks that issued this money could not claim the privilege of extinguishing their debts by offering, in effect, their own IOU's in payment. They were compelled by law to redeem their fiduciary money in international commodity money, at a fixed and unchanging price, upon the simple request of fiduciary-money holders.

They were greatly helped, in discharging this responsibility, by the reflux into their reserve coffers of the gold moneys previously dispersed in circulation and in the cash reserves of deposit banks. As indicated above, this process was accelerated after World War I by the final demonetization of gold in the domestic monetary circulation of every country in the world. This end of the process, however, also dried up inevitably one of the sources that had fed the growth of the international gold-reserve pool. The further growth of this pool now became totally dependent on the hazards of current gold production and of its excess over and above private absorption by the arts, industry, hoarding, and speculation.

The Evolution of International Monetary Reserves from Commodity Reserves to Fiduciary Reserves

The requirements of war finance and postwar reconstruction, however, had led to vast increases in national fiduciary issues and price levels throughout the world. Available monetary gold supplies were soon recognized as inadequate to feed the international-reserve requirements of the gold-convertibility system, which had reconciled, up to then, the growth of national fiduciary issues with the preservation of an international system of payments at fixed gold prices and exchange rates. A succession of international monetary palavers, culminating in the marathon debates of the luckless "Gold Delegation of the Financial Committee of the League of Nations," groped for years toward the institutionalization and internationalization of gold-convertible national currencies as an adjunct to gold reserves proper.

This so-called gold-exchange standard had grown initially in the dependent or semidependent territories of colonial powers, where monetary legislation provided for the backing of the local currencies through "international" reserves made up of the currency of the "mother country." Modest amounts of foreign exchange—primarily sterling—were also retained as "working balances" by the central banks of many independent countries, as a cheaper and more convenient way than gold to carry out day-to-day stabilization interventions in the foreign-exchange market. A further extension of the system also developed, more or less haphazardly, after World War I, as countries in need of "stabilization loans" could negotiate these more easily if they committed themselves, more or less formally, to retain the proceeds of such loans in the currency of the lending country until needed and used for balance-of-payments settlements. Finally, the acquisition of foreign-exchange balances by central banks was also spurred on by the attraction of interest earnings and by the fact that the central banks, which had been forced to suspend "temporarily" convertibility in the aftermath of the war, were barred by their monetary legislation from buying or selling gold—but not foreign exchange—at any price different from the now theoretical prewar gold parity of their national currency.

Thus it is that the "fiduciary" concept jumped the national borders and penetrated the *international* reserve system in the form of purely *national* fiduciary currencies. In spite of the major crisis, which all but wiped it out in the early 1930's, and of the recurrent sterling and dollar crises of recent years, the uneasy marriage of gold holdings and national fiduciary currencies (sterling and increasingly dollars) still characterizes the gold-exchange standard of today. It parallels the early phase of fiduciary money in national monetary systems, that is, the uneasy coexistence of commodity money with currency or deposit money liabilities, freely issued by separate deposit banks but convertible at any time into commodity money by the issuing institutions. Even the current negotiations on international monetary reform still shy away from the conclusion strongly suggested by this historical precedent, that is, the need to concentrate into a single depository institution, capable of orienting their global amounts, the fiduciary reserves held, alongside gold, by participating central banks. Still more remote from consideration is the next evolutionary phase in which such fiduciary reserves will fully substitute for gold itself, bound to be demonetized ultimately, internationally as it has long been nationally. Note that even this long-term prospect would only involve the adoption of a single reserve medium for *international* settlements between *national* central banks. It would not involve, in any way, the worldwide acceptance of a single currency issued by a supercentral bank. The payments media circulating in the public would remain national currencies, issued under the control and responsibility of national monetary institutions whose policy failures would continue to be sanctioned by payment difficulties and, eventually, variations in the exchange-rate pattern. Full currency mergers can hardly be realistically envisaged for many years to come, except within the narrower confines of *regional* integration, such as foreseen in the

Central American Monetary Union Agreement and proposed as a still somewhat distant goal for the European Economic Community.

The International Adjustment Mechanism

The other major line of development of the last twenty years is the unprecedented and rapid growth of postwar efforts aiming at ensuring the intercompatibility of national monetary policies in a growingly interdependent world.

The need for such conscious coordination of national policies did not arise in any acute form previous to World War I, this coordination being then sufficiently enforced by market forces themselves. The convertibility of fiduciary money into commodity money imposed, in those days, a rough harmonization of the rates of credit expansion of all money-creating banks, irrespective of national borders. Central banks themselves were not immune from such market forces as long as their policy horizon was confined to preserving the convertibility of their own monetary liabilities into gold money, for domestic circulation as well as for settlements beyond the country's borders (see Chapter 1).

The situation changed radically, however, after World War I, and particularly under the spur of the world economic crisis of the 1930's. Central banks were led, or forced, by deep-rooted social and political pressures, to finance, through their monetary issues, national policies of war-waging at first, of economic reconstruction afterward, and finally of full, or at least acceptable, rates of employment and economic growth. Such policies had to be pursued, even if they entailed legal relief from their convertibility obligations through the imposition of various techniques of trade and/or exchange restrictions, or through exchange-rate readjustments.

These new techniques of *external* balance-of-payments adjustment were overwhelmingly guided at first by purely nationalistic considerations, and played havoc with the international trade and exchange system. Retaliation and beggar-my-neighbor policies spread from one country to the other and dragged them all into the vicious spiral of competitive deflation, devaluations, and restrictions of the disastrous decade of the 1930's.

The tragic lessons of this period have inspired the largely successful efforts undertaken after World War II to restore a workable harmonization of national rates of monetary and credit expansion, not through an impossible return to nineteenth-century laissez faire, but through conscious efforts to define and implement mutually compatible national policies. Frequent and virtually continuous confrontations of, and consultations on, the policies of persistent deficit or surplus countries are carried out in such forums as the IMF, the OECD (the OEEC of former days), the Monetary Committee of the EEC, and so on. Financial assistance is made available to support agreed-upon policies, and nonretaliation by other countries is assured to the deficit country that finds itself unable to eschew devaluation or temporary restrictions, as long as this inevitability is recognized by others and made subject to adequate consultations with them on the ways and means to speed up the return to exchange-rate stability and to the trade- and exchange-liberalization commitments mutually accepted by all member countries.

This international consultative machinery still leaves much to be desired. Pressures are easier to apply on the deficit countries in need of external assistance to reconstitute depleted levels of international reserves than to the surplus countries. Reserve-center countries, such as the United Kingdom in former days and the United States today, may also escape for long the disciplinary impact of reserve losses through the willingness of foreign central banks to accumulate their IOU's as reserves. On the other hand, the massive cashing of such IOU's into gold metal—for financial or political reasons—runs the risk, at a later stage, of bringing unbearable pressures on the reserve currencies and on an international reserve system that has become exceedingly dependent upon them.

Working Party No. 3 of the OECD is now debating the ways and means through which growing concern with the defects of the present international adjustment mechanism might spur the further expansion, tightening, and institutionalization of the *ad hoc* consultative process already in existence.

Negotiating Tactics and Convergent Interests

Negotiations on these two major problems—the international reserve system and the international adjustment mechanism—entered an active phase with the formation of the Group of Ten in October, 1963. Their achievement to date is impressive indeed. A rare unanimity has been reached at the official level on the diagnosis of the defects of the system and even on the broad principles that should inspire the revolutionary reforms required to adjust it to the economic needs that it should serve.

Concrete agreements and commitments on the practical implementation of these principles, however, have been blocked so far by the usual habit of diplomats to lose sight of the *convergent* interests of their countries and their people—even if they constitute 90 percent of the issues at stake—and to concentrate their attention instead on minor *divergences* of interests, real or fancied, enshrined into national "negotiating positions" mutually incompatible with one another. The protracted bargaining that follows may then lead, at worst, to total failure, or be overtaken by events such as happened to the luckless Gold Delegation predecessors of the present Group of Ten in September, 1931. Even if this can be avoided, and agreement rescued in time, it is likely to be around some limping compromise, shaped by the hazards of the "negotiating" or even "bluffing" positions initially adopted and of the unforeseen meanderings of the haggling process that finally succeeds in eliminating, or hiding, their incompatibility. Thus:

1. The CRU proposals were initially, and openly, designed to "freeze out" the developing countries from any participation whatsoever in the reserve-creating process, lest they impart to it an inflationary bias toward excessive reserve crea-

tion and deficit financing. This point of view later proved untenable, but by that time the CRU device had become too deeply entrenched in the negotiations to be abandoned, even though it was no longer regarded as acceptable by the very country that had originally proposed it. Its main impact was exactly the opposite of what had been intended. Instead of freezing out the developing countries, it whetted their appetite for participation in the distribution of the "manna from heaven" that the Group of Ten had first hoped to monopolize for its own members.

2. One of the main obstacles to agreement among the Ten themselves has been the insistence of the United States to preserve intact the role of the dollar as a reserve currency, even though this has now become one of the main sources of the gold losses, which are of such concern to it. (Longer years of sad experience have finally persuaded the United Kingdom to take a saner view of its national interest and to seek instead to extricate sterling from similar responsibilities.) The United States involved itself thereby into a "squaring-of-the-circle" search for a new reserve asset more attractive than gold, but less attractive than unguaranteed dollars. Other countries objected to the political implications of the unregulated acceptance of dollar IOU's as international reserves, as well as to the potential frustration, which such a "privileged" status would entail, of the "multilateral surveillance" of the adjustment process.

3. One of the few agreements finally reached was a most bizarre one indeed. United States and/or United Kingdom deficits are denounced as a dangerous and unacceptable way of feeding world liquidity and both countries are urged to eliminate them. Yet, as long as they have not succeeded in doing so, any plan that might be agreed upon for the creation of a new reserve asset should be kept in mothballs, since its activation might then contribute further to the inflationary dangers attendant upon such deficits and remove pressures for their elimination. This was virtually the only point on

which both France and the United States could reach agreement with each other and with the other participating countries. An unacceptable system of reserve creation, more and more susceptible of triggering a world monetary catastrophe, should be preserved by all as long as one of its main defects is not corrected by unilateral United States action.[1]

4. The negotiators' attention and ingenuity are now officially absorbed by a host of other, apparently technical, details, which barely conceal basic disagreements regarding the actual contents of the CRU proposals. Should the new reserve asset be made of "reserve units"? of "special reserve drawing rights"? of both? Should there or should there not be a "link to gold" in their initial allocation? in their later use in settlements? in both? Which countries need extend to the IMF lending commitments larger (by how much?) than their borrowing rights, in order to assure the multilateral usability or convertibility of the "special reserve drawing rights" in the face of an unpredictable pattern of future deficits and surpluses? What upper and lower "holding limits," or other guesstimate commitments, are necessary to serve the same purpose if "reserve units" are adopted in lieu of, or in combination with, "special reserve drawing rights"? Which limits need be placed on the convertibility of dollars into gold metal rather than, or in combination with, their convertibility into new reserve units? and so on.

Are all these complicated and contorted devices really necessary? I remain convinced, for my part, that the far simpler and straightforward solutions suggested by an objective analysis of the problems to be solved could rally agreement more rapidly, and along far more workable and fruitful lines, than the current attempts to search for bargaining compromises between irreconcilable, and often ephemeral, negotiating "positions" or "instructions" unrelated to the common interests of all.

---

[1] This extraordinary conclusion of the Group of Ten negotiators inspired me to write an "Appeal to the Group of Ten," the text of which appears in the Appendix of this book.

The Managing Director of the Fund expressed forcefully several years ago "the emerging consensus among the international community that the creation of international liquidity, like the creation of domestic liquidity, should become a matter of deliberate decision." And the Group of Ten also affirmed, in its very first report, the desirability of bringing "under multilateral review and appraisal the various means of financing surpluses and deficits . . . and the various means of liquidity creation." [2]

The implementation of these fundamental conclusions would require:

1. First and foremost, agreement on the fact that any form of fiduciary reserves at least—and ultimately gold reserves themselves, as long as they need be retained in the system—should be created, or destroyed, only as a result of joint, concerted decisions aiming at a better adjustment of the world reserve pool to the noninflationary requirements of an expanding world economy.

2. Agreement on the nature and composition of such reserves, on the interest earnings to be attached to them, and particularly on iron-clad guarantees regarding their free use, at stable rates, in all balance-of-payments settlements among participating countries.

3. Agreement on the use to be made of the lending potential inevitably associated with the accumulation of fiduciary reserves by the surplus countries.

All three of these obvious conclusions would rule out the free and uncoordinated use of *national* currencies as *international* reserves—beyond the limits of so-called working balances—as well as their wanton cashing, at a later stage, into gold metal. If, and as long as, the provisions mentioned under (2) failed to limit the central banks' aggregate demand for gold (in preference to fiduciary reserve assets) to available supplies, specific limits on the maximum proportion of gold reserves (or, equivalently, the min-

[2] Paragraphs 25h and 37 of the *Annex Prepared by the Deputies* (1964).

imum proportion of fiduciary reserves) to total reserves would be the only alternative to a gold revaluation, unanimously and rightly rejected so far as a solution to this problem. Finally, the management decisions called for under (3) should ideally be used, within the overall limits set by (1), as a way to strengthen the adjustment mechanism, compensate for destabilizing shifts of speculative funds between major money markets, and help finance mutually agreed-upon objectives. These need not, for the reasons developed on pp. 136–139 above, be strictly limited to short-term financing, but a wider range of choice could be preserved by concentration on credits of a revolving nature and by the use of financial intermediaries, such as the IBRD and its affiliates, for longer-term operations.

The major complexities and drawbacks of the solutions contemplated in the *Emminger Report,* as compared to those suggested above, derive from a refusal to face frankly two crucial issues that cannot be indefinitely eluded or covered up:

1. The need for joint agreements (by the creditors as well as by the debtors of fiduciary reserves) on the composition of reserves, as between gold, national currencies, and the new reserve asset, to avoid (i) dangerous sources of instability in the system—through national decisions to shift from one reserve medium to another, (ii) frustration of the multilateral-surveillance and adjustment-mechanism objectives so often emphasized in the negotiations, and (iii) unacceptable surrenders of sovereignty by reserve creditors to the major reserve debtors, that is, the United Kingdom and primarily the United States.

2. The costly sacrifice of multilateral-surveillance and adjustment objectives entailed in the attempt to elude, through automatic formulas for reserve distribution, joint management decisions on the most appropriate use of the credit counterpart implicit in any accumulation of fiduciary reserves.

The initial Gold Conversion Account Agreement outlined on pp. 146–164 above would ease this suggested reorientation of the present negotiations and speed up agreement by concentrating, in a simple and flexible manner, on the first of these two issues. Agreement on the second, and more difficult, one could then be negotiated more leisurely, and would be facilitated by the experience and familiarity thereby gained with the advantages of a new reserve asset, initially created only to consolidate the present reserve system against recognized threats to its stability, but providing a simple mechanism for future reserve expansion when the need for it becomes sufficiently obvious to rally agreement among members.

Short-Run Forecasts and Long-Run Perspectives

Failing such a reorientation, the agreements that may realistically—or optimistically—now be envisaged for some time in 1968 are likely to remain extremely modest and inadequate. They might even be overtaken by sudden and major crises that could not be handled without further recourse to the precarious kind of *ad hoc* cooperation and *bilateral* credits that have propped up the present system ever since 1960, to say nothing of "voluntary" or "mandatory" restrictions on capital movements and even on current transactions by such countries as the United States and the United Kingdom.

This would not necessarily spell disaster, but would certainly slow down, or even reverse, the enormous progress that multilateral trade and exchange liberalization, financial cooperation, and policy coordination have achieved since World War II. Yet, it may be hoped that the *ad hoc* expedients and bilateral agreements adopted under the pressure of recurrent crises would create "precedents," susceptible of later institutionalization into a broader multilateral framework and facilitating further progress in the unending process of international negotiation that is slowly adjusting an anachronistic system of national sovereignties to the realities of mutual interdependence. This was indeed the path followed in the late 1940's and early 1950's, when an impotent IMF was temporarily bypassed by bilateral United States

178 / REFORM PLANS AND NEGOTIATIONS

grants and lending, under the Marshall Plan, and by a vast network of bilateral trade and payments agreements gradually multilateralized and liberalized later on, under the aegis of the Organisation for European Economic Cooperation and the European Payments Union. In the end, these pragmatic detours did not lead away from, but back to, the worldwide objectives of the IMF itself.

Long-run predictions are far easier than short-term forecasts. Reverting to the fundamental theme of this book, I boldly predict that the historical trend toward the national displacement of commodity money by fiduciary money, and toward the increasingly centralized orientation and management of the latter by national authorities, will be duplicated in the international field by a similar displacement of gold reserves by fiduciary reserves and by an increasing subordination of the latter to joint orientation and management. This evolution is already well under way indeed. Gold reserves have already dropped, for all countries taken together, from 91 percent in 1937 to 74 percent in 1949 and 57 percent in mid-1967. *Nationally* created *international* fiduciary reserves—that is, overwhelmingly dollars and sterling —constitute today as much as 42 percent of the global reserves of countries other than the two reserve centers of the system, but are down from 56 percent in 1949. Centralized reserves on the IMF have grown, on the other hand, for the same countries from one percent only of total reserves in 1949 to 7 percent at the end of 1964 and 10 percent in mid-1967.

The inadequacy of the agreements that may be reached in the present phase of the negotiations, and the new crises that may be unleashed thereby upon the world economy, would probably reverse this trend in the short run, as was the case in the early 1930's, when fiduciary reserves declined temporarily from 24 percent of world reserves in 1928 to only 5 percent following the devaluation of sterling and the dollar. They will not, however, permanently arrest a movement that is part and parcel of a far broader evolution, which only the blindest of so-called realists are unable to read in our world's history.

The displacement of commodity money by fiduciary money

and of commodity reserves by fiduciary reserves reflects the effort of man to control, instead of being controlled by, his environment in the monetary field as well as in others.

The displacement of *national* fiduciary reserves by *international* fiduciary reserves should similarly be viewed as one aspect of the adjustment of the former tribal, feudal, and national institutions through which this control could previously be asserted, to the ever-changing realities of a more and more interdependent world.

Both phenomena should be viewed in a vaster historical perspective: the long march of mankind toward its unity and a better control of its own fate.

Appendix

The following two articles, written for a broad newspaper audience, may best summarize for the hurried reader the present stage of the international monetary debate.

An Appeal to the Group of Ten[1]

Bellagio, August 10, 1966

My dear friends,

If I am to believe *Le Monde* of last July 28, your three years of labor have not been wasted. You have succeeded—with what patience against tremendous odds!—in reaching a *unanimous agreement,* not only on the diagnosis of the latent crisis of the international monetary system, but also on the essential ingredients of the *prescription* that could remedy it:

1. The gold basis of the international monetary edifice has

[1] Translated from *Le Monde,* Paris, September 11–12, 1966.

long become desperately inadequate to provide us, in a one-story building, with the living space indispensable to the legitimate (noninflationary) needs of expansion of world trade and production.

2. These transactions have nevertheless been able to find adequate shelter in the upper stories constructed, with a haste that may even have been excessive, with the materials (dollar and sterling balances) so generously put at our disposal by the persistent deficits of the United Kingdom and particularly the United States.

3. This method of construction (of feeding the liquidities that constitute the living space of central banks) is nevertheless "unacceptable." Recurrent sterling and dollar crises demonstrate the growing fragility of the materials used, in view of the growing indebtedness of the United States and the United Kingdom toward foreign central banks: the cracks in the international monetary edifice widen at each of these jolts and some stories might crumble tomorrow.

4. These two countries—and they fully agree themselves—should therefore eliminate as rapidly as possible, "or at least reduce substantially," their future deficits.

5. When they will have succeeded in doing so, a new material recognized by all as acceptable (a new reserve instrument created by mutual agreement) would therefore become indispensable to continue the construction (provide the liquidity) necessary to the expansion of the world economy.

Why, if you are in agreement on all these points, do you choose to highlight a *disagreement,* minor after all, with one of your members—France—on the opportunity to study urgently the exact composition of this new material, the use of which should be proscribed—you are in full agreement with them on that point—until the day, which still seems fairly remote, alas! when reequilibrium of the balance of payments of the United States—and Britain?—would make it necessary and permissible (noninflationary)? Would it not be possible to dispel this disagreement by dispelling the ambiguity that justifies (?) your own recommendation to postpone so dangerously the practical implementation of the new reserve instrument?

This ambiguity rests indeed on a bizarre confusion between "deficits" and "reserves." It was not the British and American "deficits" that yesterday fed world liquidity, but only "the current accumulation" of dollar or sterling balances by your central banks. Most of all, this accumulation has ceased in fact for more than a year and a half already and has even been replaced by massive liquidation of the foreign-exchange reserves accumulated in the course of previous years. If there were any doubt on this point, it could be quickly dissipated by a glimpse at the admirable statistics assembled by the IMF and published each month in *International Financial Statistics*. One easily detects in them the fact that after having accumulated, on the average, more than a billion dollars of foreign-exchange reserves per year over the five years 1960–1964, the countries of continental Europe have liquidated more than $2.5 billion of these last year and nearly $1 billion in the first four months of this year.

Do you not feel, with M. Rueff and myself, that this accelerated *decline* of the "foreign-exchange" or "reserve-currency" component—that is, essentially dollars and sterling—of the present gold-exchange standard creates a problem far more serious, and particularly more urgent, than that of planning ahead for the day when the United States finally will have recovered equilibrium? You may surely blame your French colleagues for having proposed no constructive solution to this problem, but have you proposed one yourself?

The most obvious would clearly be a general revaluation of gold. This would remove, for a while, any danger of shortage of reserves and would enable the United States to finance the repayment of its indebtedness to foreign central banks with the accounting profits that such a revaluation would entail in its case.[2]

Whatever the convictions ascribed by some to President de Gaulle and his Minister of Foreign Affairs, France has always agreed with you so far to discard such a solution. Its most eminent proponent himself—M. Rueff—concedes that it might prove catastrophic in fact if it were not carefully prepared in advance, and dangerously inflationary if it were not accompanied by the *compulsory* repayment of sterling and dollar balances inherited from the past and by a formal prohibition of their further use as reserves in the future. He willingly admits, moreover, that a triple agreement of this kind might require more time than the present situation allows us, considering the threat of a sterling crisis entailing in its wake a major crisis for the dollar itself. He declares himself ready therefore to accept "for two years the palliative proposed by M. Triffin," and even considers that in the absence of agreement on his own proposals, "the Triffin solution is the only one that could prevent a world catastrophe." [3]

Couldn't you make the same effort as M. Rueff and myself to draw conclusions from what unites you rather than from what divides you? You demonstrate everyday by your acts the *inacceptability,* "reaffirmed" in your report, and the instability of the dollar and sterling balances used in the past as construction materials for the international monetary edifice. Continental Europe withdrew last year from the building $2530 million of its foreign-exchange bricks and replaced them, up to $2305 million, by gold ingots. But only one tenth of these ingots were made of new gold dug from the earth or bought from the U.S.S.R. Nine tenths were taken from other parts of the building itself, that is,

[2] It would, however, produce no such revaluation profits for Britain, whose indebtedness in *gold-valued* dollars to the IMF is practically equal to its gold-metal reserves. The repayment of sterling balances could nevertheless be financed, according to M. Rueff, with the revaluation profits of *other* countries, a portion of which would be earmarked for the financing of a twenty-year loan to be granted by them to Britain for this purpose.

[3] These quotations are taken from the interviews of M. Rueff by Roger Priouret in the July 6, 1966 *Figaro* and by Michel Gabrysiak in the *Sunday Times* of July 3, 1966 and *L'Aurore* of July 4, 1966.

from the gold stock of the United States and of international institutions. You may possibly strengthen thereby the walls of the European stories of the edifice but at the cost of a growing weakening of the foreign-exchange foundations that prop up the whole building.

Before concerning yourselves so much with the future construction of new upper stories, devote yourselves first to the consolidation of the stories upon which you are obliged to build. Replace by more stable materials, selected and accepted by all, the bricks that you regard as fragile and improper. This should be the main purpose justifying and requiring indeed the creation of a new reserve instrument, not in the distant future, building the edifice higher and higher, but immediately to prevent its collapse.

Since available supplies of new gold are incapable of playing this role, agree among yourselves on the nature of the instrument necessary to replace the foreign-exchange reserves that your very acts prove that you wish to discard. As for the future, "the future does not belong to anybody . . . the future belongs to God." Admittedly the conservative measures upon which you may reach agreement today do not resolve all the problems of the future. You will still have to solve tomorrow the problem of the persistent deficits of Britain and the United States and the problem of the future expansion of international liquidity. You would nevertheless have contributed to the solution of these problems:

1 . By limiting the gold losses of the United States and England to the financing of their current deficits without adding to them—as you do now—the further drains resulting from sudden and massive liquidations of a monetary indebtedness inherited from past deficits accumulated under a gold-exchange standard unanimously accepted at that time by all of you.

2 . By braking in that way the gold and foreign-exchange speculation which is responsible for a portion of the British deficits and for the near-totality of American deficits from

October, 1960, until the recent escalation of war operations in Vietnam.

3. By familiarizing yourselves with a new reserve instrument that might possibly be adopted—or adapted—to increase, as well as to consolidate, the present level of world reserves whenever you will agree on the necessity of doing so.

As to the *mergers* of national sovereignties required by such an agreement, they are no more revolutionary than those to which the functioning of the European Payments Union and the International Monetary Fund have long accustomed you. They might even be facilitated by a decentralization of the IMF decisions and operations, taking full advantage of the existence and development of regional cooperation (BIS, EEC, Central American Monetary Union, and so on). They would in any case be concerted rather than erratic, and infinitely more modest and acceptable politically than the total *surrenders* of national sovereignties to the banking and political authorities of the United States and Great Britain that are entailed by the present gold-exchange standard.

Going It Alone in Monetary Reform

The temptation to "go it alone" in international monetary reform is mounting. It is reflected not only in the ill-considered blasts emanating from our two largest banks, but also in the advice recently tendered to Congress by some academicians as well as in the ultimatum issued to the Europeans by the Secretary of the Treasury. Mr. Fowler emphasized that, in the absence of cooperation, we might feel unable to avoid "unilateral action . . . undermining the international monetary system" by subjecting it "to radical and undesirable change."

SOURCE: Robert Triffin, "Going It Alone in Monetary Reform," *The New York Times,* April 29, 1967. © 1967 by The New York Times Company. Reprinted by permission.

UNILATERAL DECISIONS

This strong reminder of the consequences of delay may have been meant to spur agreement. Unfortunately, it was coupled with a spelling out of "cooperation" in terms which are least likely to evoke it; indeed, it might be taken by other countries as confirming General de Gaulle's worst suspicions about America's monetary imperialism and its determination to exact from pliable partners, in the name of multilateral cooperation, the full underwriting and financing of policies unilaterally decided by Washington or American business interests.

Secretary Fowler specifically called for European financing of American investments and of the foreign-exchange costs of our troops and those of our allies. Read in conjunction with his speech at the International Monetary Fund last September, this could be misinterpreted as suggesting that the Europeans must retain any amount of dollar IOU's flowing to them as a consequence of the huge deficits associated with the extraordinary spurt of American direct investments in Europe—running at more than ten times the level of the 1950's—and with the unpredictable consequences of our military ventures in Vietnam.

I feel sure that this was not intended, but neither is it barred by glib academic talk about forcing the rest of the world into the dollar area, nor by recent bilateral negotiations of our highest officials aimed at extracting open-end commitments to refrain from any conversion into gold, not only of the dollars which foreign countries had accumulated in the past, but also of any dollars which might accrue to them in the future.

This conversion problem is the critical question in the esoteric debate of economists about international monetary reform.

The days of the gold standard have long been numbered. Gold is bound to be gradually demonetized internationally, as it has long been nationally.

But the alternative to the gold standard is not a dollar standard unilaterally run and managed by the United States alone, but a true international standard, calling for concerted decisions and management by all participating countries.

Americans may be understandably irritated today by the negative—or even destructive—character of some of the French actions and proposals concerning the problem. We are sorely tempted to ignore even their most legitimate objections to our own proposals and to trust in our ability to isolate them—or let them isolate themselves—from their partners in the European Economic Community. But however justified our impatience, emotions are a bad guide to policy.

FORCED INTO DOLLAR AREA

Bilateral negotiations, backed up by the threat of unilateral action, might well succeed in forcing many more countries into the dollar area than unilateral action by Britain forced into the sterling area in 1931. This would bring welcome relief from our current balance-of-payments worries, but the political cost would be high and the respite might not last long.

Gentlemen's agreements among central bankers, and even governments, to finance highly unpopular U.S. policies would be swept away, sooner or later, by dissenting parliaments and public opinion, particularly if such agreements were to endanger the survival of the European Economic Community itself. The ultimate economic, and particularly political, backlash of such policies would be unpredictable, but could hardly be attractive to any of the countries concerned.

I refuse to despair of our Administration's sanity, as well as that of our European partners when confronted with such prospects. The recent agreements among Common Market finance ministers has been widely but myopically interpreted as a victory for France, a defeat for the United States, and a setback for monetary reform. Unquestionably, continued wrangling between us and the French could have this effect, crushing an eleventh-hour chance to resume progress toward international cooperation as the only realistic alternative to going it alone.

ESSENTIAL MEASURES

But it need not be so. A more constructive attitude by the Administration to test and exploit the new negotiating opportunities opened up by the positive change in former French attitudes might lead in time to far sounder permanent reforms. But the urgent task is to gain time by concentrating first on the more modest, but essential, measures needed now, not to expand existing reserves, but to prevent their collapse through a mutually defeating gold rush by scared speculators and central bankers.

Postscript

The International Monetary Problem AFTER Rio

I am correcting the galleys of this volume upon my return from the annual meeting of the International Monetary Fund in Rio de Janeiro (September 25–29, 1967).

This historical gathering confirmed the two forecasts ventured in my manuscript, prepared approximately six months ago: A compromise agreement was finally hammered out, but along lines that reflect the hazards of an absurd negotiating process much more than the convergent interests of all in a sound organization and management of the international reserve system.

The Executive Directors of the Fund were requested by the Board of Governors to submit to them, by March 1968 at the latest, a report proposing various amendments to the Articles of Agreement and the By-Laws of the Fund, particularly with regard to the "Establishment of a Facility Based on Special Drawing Rights in the Fund." The legal instrument to be prepared by the Executive Directors will be based on a so-called "Outline" agreed upon by the Group of Ten and the IMF Executive Directors in London, on August 26, 1967.* When ready, it will be presented—by circular letter or telegram—for approval by the Board of Governors, and then to the individual governments for ratification in accordance with each country's constitutional provisions. This will involve, in most cases, action by their Congress or Parliament. The

---

* The official text of this "Outline" may be consulted most conveniently in the September 15, 1967 Supplement to the *International News Survey* of the IMF, or in Appendix to the very lucid commentary of Edward M. Bernstein in "The Contingency Plan for a New Reserve Facility," *Quarterly Review and Investment Survey* of Model, Roland, and Co. (Fourth Quarter, 1967).

proposed amendments will enter into force three months after the Fund has communicated, to its members, their acceptance by three-fifths of the members, having four-fifths of the total voting power.

The countries of the European Economic Community insisted forcefully, both in London and in Rio, on the "link" between the proposed Special Drawing Rights and other amendments and modifications to the Fund's Articles of Agreement, By-Laws, and rules and practices, which they deem essential in the light of past experience and future expectations. While this is likely to give rise still to stormy debates over the forthcoming months, I am reasonably confident that agreement will eventually be reached on this matter, as it has been on others. Most of these proposed amendments will focus on the claim of the countries of the European Community for voting arrangements giving them, as a group, the same veto power as the United States now wields on major Fund decisions alone.

My personal appraisal of the achievements and shortcomings of the Rio agreement was summarized, on the eve of the Rio meeting itself, in an article prepared for the Nihon Keizai Shimbun† *of Japan, and reproduced below with a few additional comments at the end of the text.*

The pregnancy has been inordinately long. Four years have elapsed since the launching of the official debate on international monetary reform at the 1963 IMF meeting in Washington. Everybody will be relieved, therefore, even though the Agreement delivered this week by the official midwives to an expectant world rather looks like a mere *egg,* whose hatching will still require two years, if not more, for legal drafting, approval by governments, and ratification by Congresses or Parliaments before it can come into actual operation.

Little has been done at Rio to ward off recurrent gold, dollar, and sterling crises such as those that have plagued us for the last eight years and are likely to plague us in the future as long as the United States and the United Kingdom have not succeeded in restoring a tenable balance in their international transactions. These crises will still have to be plugged *ex post* by central bank cooperation under existing bilateral "swap agreements" and by other belatedly and hastily concocted rescue operations.

The crucial achievement of the Rio meeting relates to the longer run development of a more rational reserve system. For the first time in world history, responsible officials of scores of theoretically inde-

† Reprinted with permission.

pendent and sovereign countries have agreed on the need for concerted reserve creation, deliberately oriented to satisfy legitimate—noninflationary—requirements of feasible growth in world trade and production. This is a truly momentous achievement indeed, and one that deserves full recognition by those who, like myself, feel that much more remains to be done to ensure the success of this undertaking.

The path toward a more comprehensive and meaningful agreement was blocked indeed by the inability of the negotiators to agree on the future role that the other two, and more traditional, components of world reserves (about 90 percent of the total) should play in the *overall* reserve system of tomorrow.

The first of these is monetary gold, whose supplies will continue to be governed by the hazards of gold production in the West, gold sales by the USSR, and gold purchases by speculators and by mainland China. Current and prospective supplies to monetary authorities were estimated by the IMF, a few years ago, at $700 million a year, but have barely exceeded $400 million annually over the last seven years, and have actually turned negative in the last two years, for the first time in recorded history.

The second is foreign-exchange reserves, that is, the balances in *national* currencies—overwhelmingly dollars and sterling—accumulated by central banks as *international* reserves, alongside gold itself. Their actual role in reserve creation oscillates between a maximum—about $2.3 billion in 1963, for instance—determined by the vagaries of United States and United Kingdom balance-of-payments deficits, and a minimum—*minus* $2 billion, for instance, in the first half of 1965— determined by the uncoordinated decisions of several scores of central banks to liquidate not only their current accruals of sterling and/or dollars, but even outstanding balances accumulated over many years of past functioning of the absurd Monte-Carlo roulette glorified as the "gold-exchange" standard.

The common-sense agreement reached in Rio is that gold cannot be expected to provide more than a fraction of future reserve needs, and that further piling-up of dollar and/or sterling IOU's can no longer fill the gap without raising strenuous objections against the indefinite financing of the large and persistent United States and/or United Kingdom deficits implied in such a "system." These objections have recently spilled over from the economic field to the political field, following the United States claim for such financing as an indispensable contribution to "our fight for freedom" in Vietnam on the part of countries which may strenuously disagree with our policies, or lack of policy, in this respect.

While the need for a new reserve asset—or, at least, reserve "facility"—is now unanimously recognized, some countries suspect us of wishing to have it used mainly as a substitute for gold, and a way to force them to extend in this form the international credits which they are no longer willing to extend to us directly through the acceptance and retention of the dollar balances tendered to them in settlement by other countries as well as by ourselves. They are more interested themselves in substituting—at least gradually—the new reserve asset for unrequited dollars and sterling rather than for gold in which they see the last refuge of their monetary sovereignty against the threat of dollar imperialism.

General agreement on sensible and viable reforms of our anachronistic world monetary system will remain out of reach until we agree on a more comprehensive approach, encompassing the respective role to be assigned in the future to *all three* components of world reserves, that is, to gold and foreign exchange as well as to collectively created reserve assets.[1] Such a comprehensive plan should include reasonable safeguards for the United States and the United Kingdom against unbearable conversions of old dollar and sterling balances into gold metal, while preserving their full liquidity for balance-of-payments settlements. This would require, however, as a necessary *quid pro quo* some agreed limitation on the right of reserve-center countries to resurrect the same problem again by financing their future deficits through renewed accumulation of dollar and sterling balances by foreign central banks. We have unfortunately preferred so far to trust to the opposite policy of resorting to our enormous financial, economic, and political bargaining strength to bilaterally induce other countries to apply "voluntary restraints" on their conversions of new as well as old dollars into gold metal. Such tactics may succeed in the short-run, and have indeed proved remarkably successful this year in slowing down our gold drain. In the long, or even medium run, they are bound, however, to elicit increasing bitterness and resistance abroad and to endanger the financial, economic, and even political cooperation which has proved so successful in the postwar years, in sharp contrast with the gloomy history of the 1930's nationalistic, beggar-my-neighbor policies.

[1] This problem was last debated between academics and officials at Bellagio in June, 1967. See my article on "The Coexistence of Three Types of Reserve Assets," *Banca Nazionale del Lavoro Quarterly Review* (June, 1967), pp. 107–131.

Fortunately, or unfortunately, the sterling and/or dollar crises that are most likely to recur again over the forthcoming months will require new salvage operations and should induce the United States and the United Kingdom, as well as their prospective lenders, to reopen the coexistence problem which they have so far tried to sweep under the carpet. The problem of sterling balances is also recognized now as one of the major issues in the British application for admission into the European Economic Community. Its most obvious solution, and the one most beneficial to *all* concerned parties, would be along the lines suggested on page 69, but which might also be recast provisionally into an agreement between the United Kingdom and the European Community as long as the United States continues to fight a rear-guard battle against its own true interests in this matter. Such a solution of the sterling problem, however, could not fail to stimulate also renewed interest in a broader agreement covering the reserve role of the dollar as well as of sterling in the worldwide framework of the IMF.

These are good reasons to hope, therefore, that some progress will be made on this front before the Rio agreement is ready for activation, some two years from now.

The Rio Agreement should also, in time, be improved by restoring the traditional link, which it purports to break, between reserve creation and development financing (see pp. 137–139, above). One of the main objections raised against such a link was based on the mistaken view that the *liquid* monetary obligations of the IMF could not be properly invested in *long term* assets. If this view had any shade of validity, the Rio solution would sin far more against it than my own proposals, since 70 percent of the Special Drawing Rights to be created will never have to be repaid at all. They are indeed very close to the "consols" mentioned, as the most extreme of my proposals, on p. 66 above.

In any case, the automatic allocation of the new Drawing Rights in proportion to IMF quotas is as indefensible economically as it is morally. It assigns about one third of the total to two countries alone —both among the richest in the world—and about three fourths to the developed countries, leaving the 82 less developed countries of the Fund to share little more than one fourth of the total amount. Any automatic system of allocation contravenes, moreover, the sacrosanct principle repeatedly affirmed by the Group of Ten: that is, the need to link the creation of new reserve assets to the strengthening of the balance-of-payments adjustment mechanism. Can one seriously believe that countries would be willing to underwrite indefinitely, through the automatic distribution of drawing rights, persistent deficits ascribable to policies with which they fundamentally disagree, whether economically or even politically—such as, for instance, our present war escalation in Vietnam?

Fortunately, the Rio Agreement on automatic distribution of Special Drawing Rights is limited to the first five years of operation of the new system. It should be revised at the first opportunity to earmark this new lending potential of the IMF for the support of *agreed* policies rather than of *unilateral* national policies. These agreed policies could encompass a wide variety of objectives, such as national stabilization policies, development financing, etc., including—why not? —peacemaking activities of the United Nations.

An early opportunity for amendment may be provided by another resolution, initiated by France and fourteen French-speaking African countries, and unanimously adopted at the Rio meeting. This resolution calls for a study of the conditions in which IMF, IBRD, and IDA could participate in the elaboration and financing of suitable mechanisms for price stabilization of primary products at a remunerative level. This could indeed be one, among many others, of the collective objectives to which the lending resources derived—as a by-product—from collective reserve creation could be assigned in the future.

Finally, future amendments to the Rio Agreement should ease the awesome task of collective decision making in this field by decentralizing somewhat the responsibilities of the IMF through their systematic coordination with the regional economic and monetary groups and organizations now emerging in various parts of the world (See pp. 143–146, above). This should also facilitate cooperation between such groups across a—let us hope—vanishing "iron curtain" and facilitate in time the reintegration of Eastern Europe and the USSR in the world economic community.

These, however, are tasks for the future. Rio will be a success only if we all regard it as a starting point rather than a dead end, and as opening toward further evolution of the world monetary system a path long blocked until then by the age-old myths and taboos of conservative bureaucrats and nationalistic politicians.

Selected Bibliography on the Current Debate on International Monetary Reform

I. MAJOR OFFICIAL DOCUMENTS:

  A. Issued by the International Monetary Fund:

   1. *International Reserves and Liquidity*. Washington, D.C., 1958.
   2. *Annual Report 1963* (pp. 39–52), *1964* (pp. 24–39), *1965* (pp. 9–19), and *1966* (pp. 9–20).
   3. *Summary Proceedings, Annual Meeting,* particularly *1963, 1964, 1965,* and *1966.*

  B. Issued by the Group of Ten:

   1. Secretary of the Treasury of the United States on Behalf of the "Group of Ten" Members of the Fund. *Statement* Issued on October 2, 1963; reproduced in *Summary Proceedings, Annual Meeting, 1963.* Washington, D.C.: International Monetary Fund, 1963, pp. 285–286.

2. *Ministerial Statement of the Group of Ten and Annex Prepared by Deputies.* August 10, 1964.
3. *Report of the Study Group on the Creation of Reserve Assets.* May 31, 1965.
4. *Group of Ten Communiqué of Ministers and Governors and Report of Deputies.* July, 1966.

C. Other:

1. *The Balance of Payments Adjustment Process.* Paris: Organisation for Economic Cooperation and Development, August, 1966.
2. *International Monetary Issues and the Developing Countries.* New York: United Nations, 1965.
3. *International Monetary Reform and Latin America,* Report of the CIAP [Committee on the Alliance for Progress] Group of Experts. Washington, D.C.: Panamerican Union, 1966.

II. OTHER SELECTED PUBLICATIONS:

A. From an International Study Group of Thirty-two Economists, meeting parallely to the Group of Ten, and occasionally with some of their representatives, in Bellagio, Princeton, and Zurich:

1. *International Monetary Arrangements: The Problem of Choice.* Princeton, N.J.: International Finance Section, Princeton University, 1964.
2. William Fellner, Fritz Machlup, Robert Triffin, and eleven others. *Maintaining and Restoring Balance in International Payments.* Princeton, N.J.: Princeton University Press, 1966.

B. Two extremely different comprehensive studies which I would regard as the best general surveys—the first for economists, the second for a broader audience—of the problem and its alternative solutions:

1. Fritz Machlup. *Plans for Reform of the International Monetary System.* Princeton, N.J.: International Finance Section, Princeton University, revised edition, 1964, reproduced with a few additions in *International Payments, Debts, and Gold.* New York: Charles Scribner's Sons, 1964, pp. 276–366.
2. Francis Cassell. *Gold or Credit? Economics and Politics of*

International Money. London: Pall Mall Press; New York: Praeger, 1965.

C. The most discussed reform plans (see also item E3, below):

1. Robert Triffin. *Gold and the Dollar Crisis*. New Haven: Yale University Press, 1960, revised edition, 1961; and *The World Money Maze: National Currencies in International Payments*. New Haven: Yale University Press, 1966.
2. Robert V. Roosa. *Monetary Reform for the World Economy*. New York: Harper & Row, 1965; and *The Dollar and World Liquidity*. New York: Random House, 1967.
3. Edward M. Bernstein, "Further Evolution of the International Monetary System." *Moorgate and Wall Street* (Summer, 1965), pp. 51–70.
4. Maxwell Stamp, "The Reform of the International Monetary System," *Moorgate and Wall Street* (Summer, 1965), pp. 5–16.
5. Friedrich A. Lutz. *The Problem of International Liquidity and the Multiple-Currency Standard*. Princeton, N.J.: International Finance Section, Princeton University, 1963.
6. Robert A. Mundell. *The International Monetary System: Conflict and Reform*. Montreal: Canadian Trade Committee, Private Planning Association of Canada, 1965; and "A Theory of Optimum Currency Areas." *American Economic Review* (September, 1961), pp. 657–665.
7. George N. Halm, *The "Band" Proposal: The Limits of Permissible Exchange-Rate Variations*. Princeton, N.J.: International Finance Section, Princeton University, 1965.
8. John H. Williamson. *The Crawling Peg*. Princeton, N.J.: International Finance Section, Princeton University, 1965.
9. Roy Harrod. *Reforming the World's Money*. London: Macmillan, 1965.
10. Jacques Rueff and Fred Hirsch. *The Role and the Rule of Gold: An Argument*. Princeton, N.J.: International Finance Section, Princeton University, 1965.
11. Robert V. Roosa and Fred Hirsch. *Reserves, Reserve Currencies, and Vehicle Currencies: An Argument*. Princeton, N.J.: International Finance Section, Princeton University, 1966.

D. A few other titles selected arbitrarily from the ever-growing flow of literature on the subject:

1. Leland B. Yeager. *International Monetary Relations.* New York: Harper & Row, 1966.

2. Harry G. Johnson. *The World Economy at the Cross Roads: A Survey of Current Problems of Money, Trade, and Economic Development.* Oxford: Clarendon Press, 1965.

3. Gottfried Haberler. *Money in the International Economy: A Study in Balance-of-Payments Adjustment, International Liquidity, and Exchange Rates.* Cambridge, Mass.: Harvard University Press, 1965.

4. Seymour E. Harris, ed. *The Dollar in Crisis.* New York: Harcourt, Brace, and World, 1961.

5. Tibor Scitovsky. *Requirements of an International Reserve System.* Princeton, N.J.: International Finance Section, Princeton University, 1965.

6. Milton Gilbert. *Problems of the International Monetary System.* Princeton, N.J.: International Finance Section, Princeton University, 1966.

7. Franco Modigliani and Peter Kenen, "A Suggestion for Solving the International Liquidity Problem." *Banca Nazionale del Lavoro Quarterly Review* (March, 1966), pp. 3–17.

8. Robert Z. Aliber. *The Future of the Dollar as an International Currency.* New York: Praeger, 1966.

9. Charles P. Kindleberger. *Balance-of-Payments Deficits and the International Market for Liquidity.* Princeton, N.J.: International Finance Section, Princeton University, 1965.

10. Xenophon Zolotas. *Alternative Systems for International Monetary Reform: A Comparative Appraisal.* Athens: Bank of Greece, 1965.

11. Ian Shannon. *International Liquidity, A Study in the Economic Functions of Gold.* Chicago: Regnery, 1966.

12. Emile James. *Problèmes monétaires d'aujourd'hui.* Paris: Sirey, 1963.

13. Pierre Tabatoni and others. *Problèmes de l'organisation monétaire internationale,* Travaux du Congrès des économistes de langue française 1963. Paris: Cujas, 1964.

14. Juan Sardá Dexeus. *La Reforma Monetaria Internacional.* Madrid: Real Academia de Ciencias Morales y Politicas, 1965.

E. Other bibliographical suggestions: Besides the standard economic journals and abstracts, here and abroad, readers should also consult:

1. James M. Botts. *Bibliografia sobre la Reforma Monetaria Internacional*. Caracas: Banco Central de Venezuela, 1966.
2. Martin L. Loftus. "The International Monetary Fund, 1962–1965: A Selected Bibliography," *International Monetary Fund Staff Papers*. Washington, D.C.: International Monetary Fund, November, 1965, pp. 470–524. (Past and future issues of the *Staff Papers* should also be consulted for other similar bibliographies by Dr. Loftus, and significant articles on international monetary reform, particularly by J. Marcus Fleming and Oscar L. Altman.)
3. Herbert G. Grubel. *World Monetary Reform, Plans and Issues*. Stanford, Cal.: Stanford University Press, 1963, provides a convenient selection of major official and academic contributions.
4. The Joint Economic Committee of Congress and various Subcommittees (particularly Representative Henry S. Reuss' Subcommittee on International Exchange and Payments) have published numerous *Reports* and *Hearings* containing some of the best discussions of the problem by official, academic, and business economists, as well as by the Committee members.

A selective list is given in my book *The World Money Maze*, pp. 234–235, and the full list is kept up-to-date in the *Committee Publications and Policies Governing Their Distribution*.

The last *Hearings* to have come out since then were published under the title *Contingency Planning for U.S. International Monetary Policy*. Washington, D.C., 1966.

P.S.: Two other publications, too recent to be included in the above list, are particularly worthy of attention:

1. Randall Hinshaw, ed. *Monetary Reform and the Price of Gold*. Baltimore, Md.: The Johns Hopkins Press, 1967.
2. Report of the Subcommittee on International Exchange and Payments of the Joint Economic Committee of Congress: *Guidelines for Improving the International Monetary System —Round Two*. Washington, D.C., 1967.

(Readers are urged to consult, also, the Table of Contents, pp. xiii–xvii.)

Adjustment mechanism: defects, 182; evolution, 170–172; external impact, 82–88; historical reappraisal, 5–16, 39–40; interest rate changes and, 4, 8–9, 12–13, 15, 80; internal impact, 79–82; international pace of, 16–28, 40–49; in monetary reform, 139–143; reserves and, 39–40; summary, 13–16; and supplies-to-needs adjustment, 98–99; theory, 4–5
Aliber, Robert Z., 37, 200
Altman, Oscar L., 201
Ansiaux, Hubert, 115, 135
Articles of Agreement (IMF), 123, 136

Balance-of-payments adjustment, *see* Adjustment mechanism
Balance-of-payments aftermath of World War I, 29–32; and of World War II, 32–38
Bank deposits, *see* Credit money
Bernstein, E. M., 87, 111n, 126n, 199

Blessing, Karl, 115
Bloomfield, Arthur I., 7, 12
Botts, James M., 201
British economy, after World War I, 30–32, 34–35

Callaghan, James, 116
Cash settlements, and Reserve Center, 62–64
Cassel, Gustav, 16–17
Cassell, Francis, 198–199
Central American Monetary Union Agreement, 170
Central banks, exchange market intervention of, 79–88
Charon, Jean E., viiin
Colombo, Emilio, 115
Commodity money, 19–28, 54, 76, 165–167, 178
Commodity reserves, 19–28, 55, 77, 139n, 168, 178–179
Composite reserve units (CRU), 110–

113, 117–119, 122, 125–129, 139–140, 172–174

Convertibility, 15–16, 29–32, 55, 79, 88–89, 99–102

Coombs, Charles A., 36

Credit money, 19–28, 54–55, 76–77, 165–167, 178

Credit operations: and Reserve Center, 64–68; transitional, 69

Credit reserves, 19–28, 77, 168–170, 178–179

CRU, *see* Composite reserve units

Currency notes, *see* Credit money

Currency reserve balances, consolidation of outstanding, 69

Deflationary bias, 81–82, 140–143

de Gaulle, Charles, 108, 113, 184

Demand deposits, *see* Credit money

Dexeus, Juan Sardá, 200

Dillon, Douglas, 38

Discount rates, 8–9, 12–13, 15, 80

Ellsworth, Robert F., 147n

Emminger, Otmar, 110

Emminger Report, 110, 116–117, 122–123, 176

European Economic Community (EEC), 111–112, 118–119, 132, 170, 191

Exchange rates: flexible, 82n, 105; floating, 73–74; managed, 74–75; and reserve increases, 88–89; stable *vs.* fluctuating, 72–75

Fellner, William, 40n, 82n, 198

Fiduciary money, 40–42, 79, 165–170, 178; *see also* Credit money

Fiduciary reserves, 168, 175–176, 178–179; *see also* Credit reserves

Flemming, J. Marcus, 201

Foreign exchange, reserves and, 99–102

Fowler, Henry, 116, 118, 186–187

Friedman, Milton, 73, 93

Fromm, Erich, 75

Fund units, 125–129 *passim*

Gabrysiak, Michel, 184n

General Arrangements to Borrow (GAB), 113, 120, 122, 136, 139, 156, 158–159

Gilbert, Milton, 200

Giscard d'Estaing, Valéry, 108

Gold Conversion Account, 150–164 *passim,* 176–177; agreement, text of proposed, 162–164; International Monetary Fund and, 159–160, 162; reserve increases and, 159, 164

Gold-exchange mechanism, in reserve creation, 88–102

Gold-exchange standard, 56–57, 84–88, 168–169

Gold production, 18–19, 22–29, 41–43, 83, 96–98

Gold reserves, 96–98, 178; *see also* Commodity reserves, Gold production

Gold standard: adjustment, international pace of, 16–28; adjustment mechanism, 4–16; death of, 54–55; evolution, 76–77; inadequacy of, 182; Reserve Center and, 63–64; *see also* Adjustment mechanism

Group of Ten, 21, 90, 102, 104–128 *passim,* 130–134 *passim,* 139, 147, 150, 172–175, 181–186, 190, 197–198

Grubel, Herbert G., 14n, 73n, 201

Haberler, Gottfried, 200

Halm, George N., 199

Harris, Seymour, 200

Harrod, Roy, 199

Hart, Albert G., 139n

Hirsch, Fred, 199

Holtrop, M. W., 114

Imlah, Albert H., 11n

Interest-rate changes, 80

International capital movements, 9–12

International Monetary Fund (IMF), 44–45, 89–90n, 96–98, 104–109 *passim,* 112–129 *passim,* 177–178, 186, 197; annual meeting, 1967, 190–192; Articles of Agreement, 123, 136; credit operations, 136–139; foreign-exchange reserves and, 192; Gold Conversion Account and, 159–160,

162; in gold crisis of 1960, 36–38; and monetary reform, 119–124, 131n, 135–149 *passim*, 154

International monetary reform, *see* Monetary reform

International monetary system: evolution, 167–170; gold standard, 1815–1913, 3–28; reform, 156–157; after World War I, 29–32; after World War II, 32–38

International reserves, *see* Reserves

James, Emile, 200
Johnson, Harry G., 200
Johnson, Lyndon B., 113

Kaldor, Nicholas, 139n
Kenen, Peter, 200
Kindleberger, Charles P., 200
Kitchin, Joseph, 16n
Kondratieff, N. D., 17, 19

Lederer, Walther, 87
Liquidity, unconditional, 120–124
Loftus, Martin L., 201
Lutz, Friedrich A., 199

Machlup, Fritz, 40n, 82n, 93n, 137, 198
Maddison, Angus, 6n
Maudling, Reginald, 162
McKinnon, Ronald I., 72
Meade, James, 74
Mendes-France, Pierre, 139n
Mertens, Jacques E., ixn, 76–77
Mitchell, B. R., 7n
Modigliani, Franco, 200
Monetary deficit, 80, 82, 83, 87
Monetary expansion, 21–24, 55–56
Monetary institutions, evolution of, 53–60
Monetary reform: adjustment mechanism, 139–143; alternatives to, 70–77 *passim;* basic features, 61–70; and cash settlements, 62–64; composite reserve units and, 139–140; credit operations, 64–68, 136–139; currency-reserve balances and, 69; exchange rates and, 72–75; forecasts,

177–178; of gold standard, 63–64; Group of Ten and, 130–134 *passim*, 139, 147; international guarantees and, 69–70; International Monetary Fund and, 131n, 135–146 *passim*, 191; national policies and, 78–88; national sovereignty and, 70–72; negotiations, 103–129; objections to, 70–77 *passim;* objectives, 131–146; Ossola Report, 130–136 *passim;* other issues, 70–77 *passim;* participants in, 134–136; past evolutionary trends, 58–60; and regional monetary integration, 143–146; Reserve Center and, 62; reserve creation and, 131–136 *passim;* Rio Agreement, 190–195; unilateral, 186–189; *see also* Negotiation

Monetary reform proposals, 146–162; broad features, 149–152; and creditors, 152–154; and debtors, 154–156; by Group of Ten, 147, 150; incentives for, 146–148; International Monetary Fund and, 147–149 *passim*, 154; international monetary system and, 156–158; negotiability of agreement, 152–156; other proposals, 161–162

Monetary surplus, 80, 82–83, 87
Monetary systems, development of, *viii–x*
Monnet, Jean, 145
Mundell, Robert A., 86, 199

National banks, *see* Central banks
National borders, adjustment affected by, x
National monetary systems, evolution of, 165–167
National policies, mutual adjustment of, 78–88; external impact, 82–88; internal impact, 79–82
Negotiations, monetary reform, 103–129; agreement, 104–107; composite reserve units, 110–113, 117–119, 122, 125–129; compromises and dissents, 110–119; divergences, 107–110; flexible exchange rates and, 105; Group of Ten and, 104–128 *passim;* International Monetary Fund, 104–109 *passim*, 112–129 *passim;* new re-

serve assets and, 106–129; UNCTAD report, 124–129; underdeveloped countries and, 124–129
Neutralization policies, 4, 7, 8, 81
Norman, Montagu, 31, 33
Nurkse, Ragnar, 7, 80*n*

Organization for Economic Cooperation and Development (OECD), 171–172
Ossola, Rinaldo, 110, 134*n*
Ossola Report, 110, 113*n*, 127, 130–136 *passim*

Paper currency, *see* Credit money
Parallelism: in discount rates, 12–13; in trade statistics, 5–6
Paris Club, *see* Group of Ten
Price stability, 6, 16–19
Priouret, Roger, 184*n*

Regional monetary integration, monetary reform and, 143–146
Reserve Center: cash settlements and, 62–64; credit operations and, 64–68; and currency-reserve balances, 69; gold standard and, 63–64; guarantees of, 69–70; national sovereignty and, 71–72; proposed operations of, 62
Reserves: adjustment mechanism, 39–40, 98–99; composition of, 149; creation of, 38–49, 57–58, 88–89, 131–136 *passim,* 173–177, 191–193; evolution, 168–170; foreign exchange component of, 92, 99–102; Gold Conversion Account and, 158–160; Group of Ten and, 172–173; negotiations about, 106–129; pace of adjustment, 40–49; rates of increase, 92–95; ratio of, to imports, 89–92; requirements, 88–95; single center of, 62; Study Group on the Creation of Reserve Assets, 106, 110, 113*n*; sources of increase, 95–98; before World War I, 24–28; *see also* Commodity reserves, Credit reserves
Reuss, Henry S., 47*n*, 201

Rio Agreement, 190–195
Roosa, Robert V., 71*n*, 75*n*, 116, 161, 199
Rueff, Jacques, 183–184, 199

Schumpeter, Joseph A., 19
Schweitzer, Pierre-Paul, 107, 122–124
Scitovsky, Tibor, 200
Shannon, Ian, 200
Sovereignty: mergers, 186; monetary reform and, 70–72; Reserve Center and, 71–72
Speculation, remedies for, 36–38, 185
Stamp, Maxwell, 199
Stein, Jerome L., 155
Strong, Benjamin, 31, 33
Study Group on the Creation of Reserve Assets, 106, 110, 113*n*; *see also* Ossola Report
Superbank, 70
Surplus, monetary, 80, 82–83, 87

Tabatoni, Pierre, 200
*Teilhard de Chardin, Pierre, viii*n
Tinbergen, Jan, 139*n*
Treaty of Rome, 145
Triffin, Robert, 3*n*, 8*n*, 9*n*, 14*n*, 33*n*, 40*n*, 53*n*, 73*n*, 82*n*, 184, 186*n*, 198–199

Unconditional liquidity, 120–124
"Uncovered" credit money, 28
UNCTAD, 104, 139*n*, 144; report, 124–129
Underdeveloped countries, negotiations and, 124–129
U.S. economy, after World War II, 32–35
"Universal national-currencies standard," 83–88

Wage adjustment, 6–7
Williamson, John H., 199
World Bank, 126
World reserves, *see* Reserves

Yeager, Leland B., 200

Zolotas, Xenophon, 200